At
Wit's

End

D0823427

"A practical step-by-step guide for people seeking hope and help through the shadowy maze of mental illness and addiction."
—William Cope Moyers
author of *Broken: My Story of Addiction and Redemption*

"*At Wit's End* skillfully shares useful science and practice in an engaging and manageable read. When nothing is left but hope, this book is a light to stable and rewarding recovery."
—Johnny W. Allem
president/CEO of Johnson Institute

"An essential addition to addiction literature and an invaluable guide for families."
—Katherine Ketcham
coauthor of *Teens Under the Influence:*
The Truth about Kids, Alcohol, and Other Drugs and
Broken: My Story of Addiction and Redemption

At
Wit's

End

What You Need to Know
When a Loved One Is Diagnosed
with Addiction and Mental Illness

Jeff Jay
Jerry A. Boriskin, Ph.D.

616.8607
Jay

Hazelden
Center City, Minnesota 55012-0176

1-800-328-0094
1-651-213-4590 (Fax)
www.hazelden.org

Library of Congress Cataloging-in-Publication Data

Jay, Jeff, 1954 –
    At wit's end : what you need to know when a loved one is
diagnosed with addiction and mental illness / Jeff Jay, Jerry A.
Boriskin
        p. cm.
    Includes index.
    ISBN 978-1-59285-373-1 (softcover)
    1. Dual diagnosis—Patients—Mental health. 2. Substance
abuse—Patients—Mental health. 3. Mentally ill—Drug use.
I. Boriskin, Jerry A. II. Title.
    RC564.68.J39 2007
    616.86'075—dc22

                                                2006039649

11 10 09 08 07   6 5 4 3 2 1

Cover design by Dave Spohn
Interior design by Ann Sudmeier
Typesetting by Prism Publishing Center

Contents

Introduction:
The Art and Science of Hope

When mental health issues and addiction become enmeshed, we refer to them as co-occurring disorders. Examples include anxiety and alcoholism or depression and addiction to narcotic pain medication. Co-occurring disorders present a greater level of complexity in diagnosis and treatment than addiction or mental health issues alone. If we treat the alcoholism without addressing the anxiety disorder, for instance, the individual may not be able to participate meaningfully in therapy or Twelve Step groups.

This book has been written primarily for family members and friends who are trying to cope with a loved one's co-occurring disorder. Our goals are to help family members to identify what the problems are and find solutions. We will introduce the maze of professionals that families and patients will meet along the journey. We will describe the most common mental health problems and will offer insight into the best methods for addressing those problems.

People suffering from co-occurring conditions will also benefit by reading this book. As with any illness, an informed and educated patient works more effectively with the treatment team. We hope this book will bring clarity and hope, as well as provide some simple steps that will complement and enhance any formal treatment plan. By learning more, it is likely that the patient will have a speedier recovery and will be more successful in keeping the conditions in remission.

Professionals who work in the fields of mental health and addiction will also benefit from reading this book. The fact is that these two fields have been balkanized throughout most of their history and have often been at war with each other, to the detriment of the patients they serve. Our goals are to provide a clear understanding of the root of these contentions and to provide fresh insights into how clinicians from the two fields can work together most effectively. The treatment of concurrent conditions contains many paradoxical elements. We must be aware of many levels of complexity, but we must also keep the solutions simple so they can be implemented realistically. As professionals, we must rely on evidence-based medicine, but we must also inspire our patients to follow their treatment plans. It will surprise practitioners from both fields to learn how they can increase compliance, the number-one problem in treating chronic illness.

This book provides hard information, like the meaning of a diagnosis such as bipolar II. It also provides guidance, including how to evaluate a treatment plan. Finally, it provides case histories that show how families, patients, and treatment teams deal with problems and find solutions. So this book will provide knowledge, direction, and hope.

There continues to be controversy in the treatment of co-occurring disorders, even among clinicians at the same treatment center. Some argue for the primacy of mental health issues over everything else, where others claim that mental illness will almost always subside once the addict achieves sobriety. One of our goals in this book is to bring clarity to this controversy, based on the latest research and decades of firsthand clinical experience.

Part of the dilemma that clinicians face is that the human condition contains a wide spectrum of emotion and feeling, from great joy and exuberance to great pain and sorrow. But we don't need to put a label of sickness on the extremes of this spectrum unless they are debilitating and ongoing. Some experts have a tendency to label and medicate every psychological ailment, but this is not necessarily helpful. For example, with many forms of depression, especially those with obvious causes, such as the death of a parent, there are few prescriptions better than daily walks, sound nutrition, adequate sleep, and time spent talking with family and friends. Such depressions, as agonizing as they are, will normally pass.

Of course, there are times when psychiatric medication is needed immediately. Active hallucinations, ongoing panic attacks, and crippling depression may all call for medical help. But this must be measured and reevaluated as treatment progresses. It is often necessary to medicate patients for anxiety in order for them to participate on any level in group therapy. However, after a period of time, they may need very little medication or none at all.

What all this means is that there are no simple answers for complex problems. The answers to a particular dilemma may change over time, but this is not so unusual. Take a badly broken leg, for example. Surgery may be required at first, followed by a restrictive cast and crutches. But these interventions are not required forever. Before long, the leg will heal and rejuvenate with the help of a less restrictive brace and physical therapy.

In the same way, patients with co-occurring disorders may need intensive help early on, including medication. But they won't always be in need of stabilization. With the help of ongoing therapy and a gradually less restrictive treatment environment, they can regain their health and normal functioning.

Co-occurring disorders are also referred to as dual diagnosis and co-occurring conditions, and some people use a more casual and less clinical name: double trouble. Regardless of what term is used, friends and family members of the dually diagnosed are often at wit's end when trying to fathom the situation, much less know what steps to take to lend some normalcy to everyday life. Addicts and the mentally ill can wreak havoc on the lives of friends and family members. When a person suffers from both, loved ones are often doubly confused and frustrated.

Many patients suffer from apathy, cynicism, and hopelessness. These maladies will never be cured by a pill, and they can't be turned around overnight. It is necessary that patients come to believe that they can get better, that their symptoms can be put into remission, and that they can develop a new vision of their lives. This new vision—a reason to move forward—is as necessary to successful treatment as any diagnosis. It is also one of the great facts of the human condition. Once a person has a powerful reason to live—whether for love, faith, friendship, or goals—the obstacles become challenges and stubbornness turns into determination.

Treating addiction coupled with mental illness is especially difficult because, at some point, patients must become active participants in the process. They must literally become their own treatment managers and primary caregivers. Unlike an acute illness such as appendicitis, which might be treated with an operation, chronic illnesses such as addiction and mental health problems require ongoing help and support. And because patients cannot be in treatment forever, they must learn to manage their own recovery. Part of the goal of treatment is to help inspire a great awakening of a patient's mind and spirit that will allow this miracle to take place. No one, whether patient, professional, or family member, can command this awakening to take place. But we can help bring all the elements together, along with a pinch of hope, faith, and determination.

The good news is that treatment works and many people are recovering today from co-occurring disorders. Interestingly, many of these people go on to help others, through various support groups in their communities. This activity often provides more meaning and satisfaction to recovering people than most of us can imagine.

War veterans are loath to talk about their combat experiences with civilians. But bring a group of veterans together for a couple of hours, let them talk about issues that are meaningful to them, and you will be hard-pressed to find a stronger fellowship. In the same way, people who have survived co-occurring disorders and have made their way into recovery are veterans of an intense battle. We have learned over the decades that they have a special gift for helping each other and that the exercise of this gift is powerful medicine.

A Note on Numbers

In this book, we will steer away from statistics as much as possible, because when it comes to dual disorders, statistics tend to obscure facts rather than clarify them. As professionals, we're often asked a simple question by families: "What is this treatment center's success rate?" Strange as it may seem, this is a devilishly difficult question to answer. Let's take a look.

If the patient—our loved one—completes treatment and stays sober and symptom free for one year, we would call him a success in our review of the first year. But what if he has a slip after seven months? What if he only stays sober for 360 instead of 365 days? Is he a success? Most people would say yes, of course. But it makes statistical analysis very difficult. At what point do we say that treatment has failed?

New tools such as the Addiction Severity Index, or ASI, have been developed to help answer this question, but they offer little comfort to families. After all, spouses and parents are not just looking for a reduction in alcohol or drug use or a reduction in psychiatric symptoms. They want their loved ones back. And that should be the goal of all treatment.

Our task is further complicated by the fact that quality treatment is somewhat like exercise equipment. The old saying is true: "It works if you work it." Therapists have many ways to engage a patient in the treatment and recovery process, but there is no magic wand. At some point, the patient must engage in the process, or even the best treatment will be fruitless. We wouldn't say a home gym didn't work because the owner never used it. In the same way, treatment isn't necessarily defective if the patient doesn't engage.

A little story illustrates the point. There was a great clinical supervisor at an inpatient treatment center who was also a recovering drug addict. He went through treatment many times before he finally began his recovery. He would often ask young counselors under his supervision, "Which one of my treatments do you think was successful?" They almost always answered, "The last one." Then he would laugh and say, "No, they all worked, but it took every one of them to make a success out of me."

Judging success in the treatment of concurrent conditions such as addiction and bipolar disorder is like judging success in chronic illnesses such as diabetes. The patient has primary responsibility, in the end, for maintaining the ongoing program of recovery. That's why patients who are involved in Twelve Step groups, outpatient group therapy, and other support systems are so much more likely to succeed, because they are not relying on themselves alone for the motivation to carry on, day in and day out. In this way, success may ultimately be judged by the patients' ability to stay connected to such a group, so they can deal with setbacks as well as achievement.

As families and clinicians, we want to keep our eyes fixed on long-term solutions. These solutions always include a mix of different elements to address the complex problems we face. There are no magic bullets, but there is a way out of the wilderness. We will help to arm families with tools, knowledge, directions, and tips. Knowing the odds won't help families, because for them there are no statistics. There is only success or the determination to keep trying.

At
Wit's

End

1

Ashley's Story

My daughter is depressed and hallucinating. She had a bad LSD trip, but she swears she is no longer using. She is seeing a psychiatrist and taking antidepressants but does not seem to be getting better. What do I do?

Ashley's mother

Ashley, an attractive honor student and high school freshman, had been going through what seemed to be typical rebelliousness. She had multiple piercings, dyed her hair, and seemed to be working toward a "cool persona." She gravitated toward a peer group that worried her parents. Her grades fell, she began sleeping in class, and she started cutting herself. She would disappear more and more often with her friends, lying about her whereabouts. She had a much older boyfriend, and her moods were unstable. Worried about her depression and behaviors, Ashley's parents insisted she begin seeing a psychologist.

One night, she did not come home. She wandered in the next morning talking gibberish, staring straight ahead, and acting paranoid and psychotic. At first she was emotional, and then she fell mute. She refused food and water. An emergency trip to the psychiatrist resulted in a weeklong psychiatric hospitalization, where she admitted she had taken LSD the night she went missing. She slowly emerged from the psychotic state and was discharged, but she continued to be depressed, paranoid, and intermittently suicidal. She argued with her parents, often picking fights. Her sleep pattern was disturbed, her concentration poor, and, in the middle of the night, she repeatedly cut herself. The cuts were slashes on her legs and torso, nonlethal but deep enough to be frightening. She was on at least four different medications and had been in and out of the hospital two additional times. The psychiatrists said she was severely depressed, perhaps psychotic, and in need of much help. They thought the drug episode might have damaged her brain, exacerbating her initial disturbance.

At a nationally renowned psychiatric facility—her third hospitalization—the possibility of addiction was mentioned. While her parents knew substance use was an issue, Ashley was so moody, irrational, and depressed that they continued to focus on her psychiatric outpatient care. Ashley denied using chemicals regularly, acknowledged occasional drug use, but insisted her problem was just depression. She swore she would never do acid again and kept her promise.

One of Ashley's friends from out of state visited her during winter break. Though still very depressed, Ashley seemed to respond well to her friend; however, on New Year's Eve, Ashley slashed both wrists. After the wounds were stapled closed, she was admitted to the hospital a fourth time and put on the psychiatric unit. Her friend told Ashley's parents that the real problem was drugs. With the friend's report, staff searched Ashley's belongings and found Ecstasy. Ecstasy is often called the "love drug"; it is an amphetamine and a hallucinogen, definitely harmful and addictive. It became apparent that Ashley, in addition to having mental health symptoms, was also a drug addict. With that information, her treatment options changed dramatically and became more complex—both the addiction and the psychiatric problems needed attention.

Ashley was transferred to a highly regarded addiction treatment program. The first day on the unit, she resumed superficial self-cutting, something most addiction programs are not prepared to handle. They transferred Ashley to a psychiatric facility and told her parents she could not return to the addiction program. In an ironic turn of fortune, Ashley was so frightened by this psychiatric facility that, in an effort to get herself out, she resolved not to injure herself again.

Ashley returned to the addiction treatment program and completed it. Meanwhile, her parents struggled to find a school environment for the then-fifteen-year-old, who needed ongoing Twelve Step work and psychiatric help. The options were few. They selected a school that appeared to fit the bill but proved to be unpleasant and incompetent. Returning home and determined to stay clean, Ashley became active in Narcotics Anonymous (NA) and Alcoholics Anonymous (AA). She was clean for a year but then got involved with an older crowd and relapsed. A quick admission to a mediocre facility permitted Ashley to reconsider her options and her recovery.

She came home hostile. She was frustrated that the facility concentrated solely on her addiction, ignoring the unpleasant symptoms that had plagued her since her first bad LSD trip. She explained that the hallucinations persisted, not in the full-blown way they had the first time, but in a way that was frightening, consistent, and intrusive. She was anxious, and these ongoing "flashbacks" were ignored by the addiction professionals and not understood by the psychiatric professionals. Ashley told her parents that the cutting behavior helped ease the anxiety from the hallucinations that plagued her, especially at night.

Upon returning home, Ashley went to an outpatient psychiatrist who tried to treat the symptoms that were ignored by the drug treatment facility. The psychiatrist placed Ashley on multiple medications at high doses, many of which created other symptoms requiring additional medications. Her desperate parents found a more conservative psychiatrist who reduced the number of medications she was taking to two—an antidepressant and a mood stabilizer. Her mood improved, as did her concentration, but the thought of returning to her old high school frightened Ashley and her parents; they feared that being around the people and places she associated with using could compromise her recovery. Ashley dropped out of high school, completed a GED, and went on to a technical college. She graduated valedictorian of her class and was also the youngest person to graduate from the program.

Ashley is the daughter of a mental health professional, a Ph.D. working in the addiction field. The story is recounted here to illustrate how difficult it can be to know what to do when faced with a blend of mental health and addiction issues. Even an experienced professional can have difficulty determining whether substance abuse and/or mental health treatment is necessary.

Ashley, who eventually discovered that helping others is part of recovery, permitted part of her story to be shared so others could learn how substances can induce psychological symptoms that linger. She is one of a growing number of young people who suffer from a syndrome known as hallucinogen persisting perception disorder (HPPD). A neglected and underreported syndrome, HPPD is the direct result of hallucinogen injury. Those who have it are more vulnerable to relapse, psychiatric misdiagnosis, and incorrect medication. It is not a widely diagnosed, researched, or understood phenomenon, yet it is becoming more common because of the popularity of hallucinogens. Even with proper treatment, psychiatric symptoms can persist.

The point of Ashley's story is to illustrate how difficult it can be to know what's going on. If a mental health professional was stumped and confused, certainly anyone can be. The purpose of this book is to better prepare families for the challenges of what is now commonly called co-occurring disorders and sometimes referred to as dual diagnosis or double trouble. Dealing with more than one issue requires a different way of thinking as well as additional knowledge. Knowing what to look for, what questions to ask, and what treatments work can save families and their loved ones from being lost in a maze of confusion.

In prior decades, mental health issues were treated by mental health professionals, and addictions were treated by addiction professionals. Today, we know that most people enter addiction treatment with a co-occurring disorder and that their treatment needs to be well rounded enough to address both issues. As Kenneth Minkoff, M.D., a leading expert on co-occurring disorders, states, "Dual diagnosis is an expectation, not an exception."

The more families learn about the overlap of these disorders, the better equipped they are to seek the best kind of help. This was Ashley's desire in permitting us to tell part of her story.

2

Finding Help

Those of us dealing with co-occurring disorders are often overwhelmed with confusion. Why is my loved one being so irrational? Why can't he follow through with his stated intentions? Why is she so dysfunctional? We all strive to answer these questions, and most of us endure bewilderment, anger, frustration, fear, and confusion in the process. Indeed, ambiguity, helplessness, and a state of chronic stress seem to surround individuals and families living with addiction and psychological difficulty. The experts are still struggling to understand each of these phenomena individually, let alone both of these conditions functioning together at the same time.

It is very difficult to know exactly what role addiction or mental illness is playing in an individual at any given time. Both conditions produce similar symptoms, yet they operate on different pathways. Assuming a certain behavior is due to an addiction when it is really caused by an anxiety disorder is an invalidating and potentially dangerous mistake. How do we get a handle on all of this? First, we need to understand some of the key components of treatments that work.

Continuum of Care

People working in the health care professions—whether heart surgeons or social workers—use the term *continuum of care* when discussing the full range of services needed to treat a patient. The continuum of care also encompasses the setting in which those services are provided, either inpatient or outpatient. For example, a person with a heart problem may be diagnosed in his doctor's office (outpatient), then referred to a surgical team for a heart bypass operation (inpatient), and then monitored by his doctor for follow-up (aftercare).

People suffering from co-occurring disorders also have access to a wide variety of services and providers, both inpatient and outpatient. As with heart patients, the most intensive services will be delivered in an inpatient setting, with outpatient follow-up. In both settings, a variety of treatment professionals will be involved with the case. In the best treatment centers, a multidisciplinary team will develop an individualized treatment plan for the patient. As the name implies, a multidisciplinary team is made up of different specialists who bring different skills and insights to the case. Just as a heart surgeon doesn't provide physical rehabilitation, a psychiatrist does not provide ongoing counseling.

In the following sections, we will introduce the different types of facilities families may encounter while seeking treatment for a co-occurring disorder. We'll describe the various roles of the professionals who work in them and give you some inside information and history about the relationships between the various professions. Finally, we'll give an example of how a good multidisciplinary team works to develop a detailed treatment plan, to deliver the services it calls for, and to help a patient get on the road to recovery.

Facilities

Different levels of care are provided in different facilities. For example, a hospital can provide more services than a doctor's office. Following are the various settings in which you will find services for co-occurring disorders and what you can expect from each.

Outpatient

Outpatient treatment may often be found in a professional office building within a few miles of your home. It is similar to going to your family doctor's office. You can receive basic diagnostic services in an outpatient setting along with ongoing therapy. It is not the preferred setting for intensive treatment; however, there is an option called intensive outpatient treatment (commonly called IOP), or day treatment, which provides a higher level of services in an outpatient setting, usually up to five days per week, three to six hours per day.

Outpatient treatment is preferred by insurance and managed care companies because it is less expensive than inpatient or residential treatment. Most outpatient therapy consists of weekly one-to-one sessions, either with a therapist or a psychologist, and it may also include group therapy. IOP services can include a mixture of group therapy, individual counseling, and education. Random drug and alcohol screening may also be included. The best providers will include a family program. Because patients return every day to their homes and schedules when they leave treatment, the opportunity to relapse during treatment is ever-present.

Outpatient treatment is most effective when used in conjunction with inpatient or residential care. It is the setting of choice for aftercare and continuing therapy following primary treatment in an inpatient or residential setting.

Inpatient Addiction Facility

Patients in an inpatient facility receive around-the-clock care in a safe environment. Patients begin their stay in the medical unit, where they go through medical detoxification (detox) and stabilization. Patients are then moved to a residential unit, where they will stay from two weeks to several months, depending on the nature of the facility and the needs of the patient. Inpatient treatment is also referred to as residential treatment or partial hospitalization.

These different names refer to technical levels of care and staffing requirements. For example, a true inpatient facility will have twenty-four-hour nursing care, whereas a residential facility may only have nurses and other medical staff available during the day. In a minority of cases, admission to an inpatient psychiatric hospital is required to stabilize acute symptoms such as hallucinations. However, this kind of care is only required to bring severe symptoms under control. Afterward, a less restrictive residential setting will likely be approved.

Inpatient Psychiatric Facility

In some instances, psychiatric hospitalization is a necessary step before addiction treatment can commence. Modern psychiatric units are designed for stabilization and evaluation, and the length of stay is usually a matter of days, although occasionally longer. While the emphasis is upon psychiatric symptoms, many facilities now evaluate and consider the role of addiction. If your loved one is imminently dangerous to self or others, involuntary commitment is sometimes necessary. The vast majority of patients enter psychiatric hospitals voluntarily. For co-occurring disorders, beginning an inpatient, residential, or intensive outpatient addiction treatment program is the next logical and often necessary step.

Aftercare

Other forms of residential care include extended care, halfway houses, and sober houses. Extended-care facilities are often an extension of primary residential treatment and offer a high level of clinical services. Extended care may be prescribed when a patient has a history of relapse, co-occurring disorders, or other concerns. Many extended-care facilities have "step-down" programs that become less restrictive over a period of months and may include part-time employment or school by the end, helping the patient to reenter society.

Halfway houses offer a clean and sober environment with some counseling services, and they require the client to be employed or to attend school. Sober houses offer the least restrictive level of care, providing a sober environment in the community but without the clinical services provided by a halfway house. Patients can access clinical services on an outpatient basis. All three of these alternatives stress involvement with Twelve Step groups as the necessary foundation for a solid recovery.

Primary treatment for co-occurring disorders should be provided by a multidisciplinary team consisting of a doctor, a psychiatrist, a psychologist, and a therapist or counselor. Ideally, the team will also include a pastoral counselor or clergyperson, a nutritionist, and a recreational therapist. Some treatment centers also offer specialty programs, such as equine therapy, ropes courses, older adult programs, and a variety of special tracks. A specific diagnosis such as trauma, for instance, might be addressed within a specialized trauma program.

Meet the Professionals

Just as there is a continuum of care for treating patients with dual diagnosis, so, too, is there a continuum of professionals that provide that care. The following is an overview of the various professions. All are critically important, but we will look at the major players in the order of their professional education.

Therapists, Social Workers, and Counselors

These professionals usually have a bachelor's or master's degree in psychology, counseling, social work, or a related field. Some, especially certified addiction counselors, often have their own personal recovery history. The primary counselors or therapists are responsible for introducing patients to the core concepts of the Twelve Steps, which provide the long-term support necessary for a full recovery.

Therapists and counselors provide the daily therapeutic regimen for the patients in a treatment center. They present lectures on pertinent topics, facilitate group therapy sessions, and provide one-to-one counseling. They are often the primary authors of the individualized treatment plan (with the other members of the multidisciplinary team) that guides the patient's progress.

In a reputable inpatient or residential facility, counselors and therapists will be closely supervised and will act as part of a team. Unless they have a master's degree, they do not usually operate as sole practitioners in an outpatient setting.

Psychotherapists and Master's-Level Clinicians

This group overlaps with the previous group in many facilities. These professionals typically have master's degrees in psychology, social work, or a related field, and they often have other certifications as well. For example, they may be LLPs (limited licensed psychologists), MFTs (marriage and family therapists), or CACs (certified addiction counselors). These professionals can work in inpatient or outpatient facilities, providing group therapy and individual counseling. Many of the better inpatient and outpatient facilities use predominantly master's-level practitioners in the roles of counselors and therapists.

Psychologists

For patients who are dually diagnosed, the doctoral-level practitioners (Ph.D. or Psy.D.) will play a critical role on the treatment team, providing psychological testing and diagnosis. Psychologists will often provide individual therapy and consultation throughout the course of treatment, dealing with trauma, depression, and other mental health issues. Psychologists work closely with prescribing doctors or psychiatrists in choosing medications that may be helpful in the treatment process.

Medical Doctors

Physicians are most actively involved with treatment during detox and stabilization. Depending on the substance or substances that have been abused, doctors will prescribe different medications to lessen the pain of withdrawal, decrease anxiety, and guard against medical problems, such as increased blood pressure. Physicians also play an important role in making sure that any additional medical issues discovered during detox, such as liver problems, are properly addressed throughout the continuum of care. Special certifications are available to physicians through the American Society of Addiction Medicine (ASAM) that ensure specific expertise with regard to addiction recovery issues.

Psychiatrists

These are medical doctors who have taken additional training and an internship in the field of psychiatry. They will provide specific medical recommendations, write prescriptions for psychiatric medications, and monitor their effectiveness. Psychiatrists are likely to see the patient less often than other professionals, but they play an important role in the medical management of mental health symptoms, and they interact closely with the treatment team.

Others

A good inpatient residential treatment center will also provide a wide variety of services to meet the spiritual, physical, nutritional, and recreational needs of the patient. As noted earlier, these caregivers include pastoral counselors or clergymembers, nutritionists, and recreational therapists. In addition, specialized diagnostic services might be provided by a neuropsychiatrist, for example.

Interventionists can also play an important role, although their involvement begins before a patient enters treatment. Interventionists are hired by families to facilitate the admission process, particularly with very resistant patients. These specialists work through a detailed process with family and friends to break through prospective patients' denial and defenses so they will accept professional help. Interventions are often necessary to get a person into treatment before a greater crisis comes along.

History

The mental health and addiction fields work together to treat patients with co-occurring disorders, but it hasn't always been that way. The two fields—addiction and mental health—have often been isolated from each other. Great strides have been made to bridge the gaps, especially through the use of multidisciplinary treatment teams, but problems still remain. To be an informed consumer of professional services for both addiction and psychiatry, it's important for you, the reader, to understand some of this history.

Until the twentieth century, alcoholism was usually seen as a moral defect. Alcoholics and drug addicts were considered bad people who were spiritually deficient, morally bankrupt, and weak willed. Until Alcoholics Anonymous came along in 1935, the most common explanation for alcoholism was that alcoholics simply lacked the willpower to stop drinking, or they were suffering from some form of schizophrenia. Neither genetics nor biology was seriously considered, and the success rate for treating alcoholism and drug addiction was dismal.

Bill Wilson and Dr. Bob Smith founded Alcoholics Anonymous (AA) in 1935, and out of their pioneering efforts came the book *Alcoholics Anonymous* (commonly called the Big Book), which provided the first complete description of the Twelve Step program.

AA transformed our view of addiction in general, and alcoholism in particular, by simplifying our understanding of the condition and developing a system that makes it treatable: the Twelve Steps. Although they are not a foolproof method for everyone, there is no denying that the Steps have helped untold millions of alcoholics and addicts. AA defines alcoholism as an illness, and this reframing of the definition of alcoholism, articulated in Step One, revolutionized American thinking about addiction. Step One assumes that addiction is a disease, a simple fact that the alcoholic is powerless to change. Paradoxically, however, this opens the door for recovery. We will devote a good deal of time to the Steps and how they can increase compliance in long-term treatment and recovery in chapter 14.

It should be noted that the concept of "powerlessness" is often misunderstood. It isn't an excuse, but rather an admission of fact: If an alcoholic drinks alcohol, her life will become unmanageable. So alcoholics are not powerless in a general sense; rather, they are powerless over the fact that they are alcoholic. The illness cannot be cured, but it can be managed through abstinence.

One of the other great revelations of AA is that once people admit their alcoholism, then and only then are they able to work through the rest of the recovery process. The importance of admitting and accepting the nature of the problem is that the alcoholic will stop blaming the condition on other people, problems, or things.

Unfortunately, during much of the twentieth century, alcoholics and addicts who sought help from psychologists and psychiatrists did not find their way to AA. Instead, they were prescribed various medications and treatments that had little chance of success. As a result, many people in the recovering community came to believe that psychology and psychiatry were "bad," and that they tended to trap people in a cycle of hopelessness.

Instead of presenting alcoholism as a hopeless, terminal condition, AA provided a system wherein alcoholics, willing to adhere to the precepts, principles, and structure of AA, stood a much better chance of recovery. Although the numbers vary, it is fair to say that the overall recovery rate for alcoholism and addiction has risen from 1 percent during the 1930s to a lifetime rate of about 33 percent today. Sobriety and longevity rates for those who strictly adhere to AA—for example, those who consistently attend meetings—are much higher, estimated to be around 80 percent. Quite an improvement for a fatal illness!

Many people who attend AA and NA (Alcoholics Anonymous and Narcotics Anonymous, the principal Twelve Step groups) have developed a prejudice against psychiatry. This is due to the abuse so many addicts endured at the hands of mental health professionals, especially in earlier decades. It was not uncommon for the alcoholic in psychiatric care to be subjected to abusive treatments. In addition, many alcoholics were treated with benzodiazepines, such as Valium or Xanax, which were all but certain to accelerate and complicate the addiction. The memories of these abuses have been repeated aloud at Twelve Step meetings (often referred to as "the rooms") as recently as the 1980s, and they continue to be repeated to a lesser extent today.

Many well-meaning AA members will say that if you are depressed or anxious, you must not be working the Steps to the fullest extent possible. However, for people with serious co-occurring conditions, AA is usually not sufficient, nor was it ever meant to be. Some forms of anxiety, trauma, and personality disorders need to be properly treated so the person is able to attend AA meetings. In the case of co-occurring disorders, the old prejudice against psychiatry in some AA meetings can undermine a person's recovery.

Now let's take a look at things from the mental health perspective, which we'll refer to broadly as psychiatry. This imperfect science came about in its younger years as a blend of philosophy, science, religion, and medicine.

Early institutions were developed to deal with a wide range of deviant behaviors that in centuries past were believed to be devil possession, witchcraft, or lunacy. Why mental illness occurred was a mystery, and there was no system of diagnosis, let alone clear, science-based treatments. Freudian theory revolutionized the treatment of mental illness by declaring it was the result of developmental problems, which at least gave the field a true theoretical footing. A long history of advances followed in the twentieth century that brought about more exacting forms of diagnosis and treatment. New techniques evolved from early analytical treatments through many forms to the modern methods of treatment we have today, such as dialectical behavior therapy. Brain research led to the development of modern psychiatric medications, and ongoing research holds tremendous promise.

But before the modern era, alcoholism was perceived as a personality disorder. With the exception of Carl Jung (who saw the condition as a problem of "spirit"), experts considered alcoholics lacking in some key developmental, bonding experience. The alcoholic could be helped only by going through deep analysis. Since most alcoholics were uncooperative and did not get better, psychiatrists looked down on them, essentially taking the moral angle. Many psychiatrists prescribed sedatives for alcoholics, which made matters worse.

For years, addiction professionals who recommended AA resented the mental health folks who prescribed medication and analysis. Mental health professionals resented addiction professionals pushing onto their turf and proclaiming that addiction was a separate condition, even a disease. To make matters worse, addiction treatment professionals often crossed the boundary into psychiatry, attempting to treat co-occurring disorders alongside alcoholism by sending people to AA. The fact that AA literature specifically states that the Twelve Steps are not meant to treat "grave emotional or mental disorders" didn't stop them. For people with co-occurring conditions, neither the addiction treatment system nor the mental health system offered a complete solution. The two fields were balkanized, not speaking to each other, and so not providing the full continuum of care. As a result, patients with co-occurring conditions usually received only half the treatment they needed, either for their addiction or their mental health problems. It was not unusual even a few years ago to find dual diagnosis patients who had had years of psychotherapy without ever having been treated for their addiction problem. Conversely, it was not unusual to hear of patients committing suicide when strident practitioners of the Twelve Steps insisted their depressive symptoms were the result of "not working the program."

But a quiet revolution has been taking place during the last fifteen years. Both fields recognize the need to join forces. The professions often work—or at least attempt to work—together. The recognition of co-occurring disorders is well under way.

One of the goals of this book is to alert readers to the dangers of overly simplistic approaches to addiction or mental illness when dealing with co-occurring conditions. It is imperative that providers be truly multidisciplinary.

Navigating the Maze

When dealing with co-occurring disorders, one of the most vexing questions tends to be "Which disorder or condition should be treated first—the mental illness or the addiction?" Assuming an ongoing addiction is coupled with a mental health issue, the answer is very easy: Begin with the addiction. Mental health issues cannot be addressed while a person is still using alcohol or drugs. However, we are not dealing with an either/or situation. Although detox and addiction treatment is the first priority, attention to the mental health issues must begin almost simultaneously. Abstinence-based treatment must commence, but at the same time diagnosis and treatment for the co-occurring psychological disorder should not be delayed. Too many addicts have relapsed or failed to thrive because the mental health issue was treated while the addiction was overlooked, or the addiction was treated and attention to the mental health issues was delayed or ignored. While the initial emphasis is upon abstinence-based recovery, often in an inpatient treatment setting, diagnosis and treatment of the co-occurring disorder must also commence, and continue during early recovery. In fact, early recovery is a time of great emotional upheaval and sensitivity. Emotions tend to be powerful and issues more accessible. It is the ideal time to correctly identify and treat the co-occurring disorders. Not too many years ago, in some communities, it was recommended that addiction be the only focal point for treatment for the first year. Currently, we recognize this puts people with co-occurring disorders at risk during early recovery. So the correct answer is treating the addiction first and initiating diagnosis and treatment for the co-occurring disorder during addiction treatment, continuing throughout early addiction recovery.

A related question is "What level of care should be provided?" Is outpatient treatment or inpatient treatment more appropriate? The level of care depends upon the severity of one or both of the disorders. Patients do not die from too much care, although inpatient treatment is not always necessary. However, if there is a true addiction, meaning that the patient will suffer significant withdrawal symptoms, inpatient medical detox and stabilization are strongly recommended. In some cases, withdrawal can be extremely uncomfortable and even fatal. Let's presume that we are dealing with a true case of dual diagnosis, with substantial mental health and addiction issues. After detox is completed, the patient will continue in residential care for a number of weeks. The treatment team will determine the course of treatment and the length of stay.

After completing inpatient treatment, it is possible that the patient will be referred to an extended-care facility, where more difficult issues will be addressed. These issues may include trauma, psychiatric disorders, or special needs. The best of these programs will offer a step-down approach that will gradually reintegrate the patient into society over a period of months. Typically, the last portion of these programs includes getting a job or doing volunteer work.

For many patients, returning home after treatment may not be the best alternative. Instead, they may benefit from going to a halfway house, in which they will continue to receive therapeutic services while they go out into the working world or school during the day. A halfway house may continue to be an important source of support for many months.

Whenever the residential portion of treatment has ended, an aftercare plan will be developed by the treatment team. This will include continued outpatient counseling, Twelve Step meetings, psychological services, and services for any other special needs that need to be addressed (for example, a medical issue such as diabetes).

It is important for families to realize that their loved ones must sign a release of information if the family is to have any chance of participating in the treatment process. It is critical that the family and significant others be able to communicate with the treatment team, first to give a thorough history of the patient's problems, and second to participate in the family program. However, if the patient does not consent in writing to this communication, the various laws of confidentiality will bar even the most rudimentary contact with the treatment providers.

We bring up this point for two reasons. First, many families wrongly believe they just need to get their loved one into treatment, and the staff will take care of the rest. In fact, both mental illness and chemical dependency are chronic illnesses, and so recovery is an ongoing process that stretches over months and years.

Second, patients are often reluctant to sign releases. They may believe that they can manipulate the treatment process if they shut out the family. This can be a real problem, because the treatment team is dependent on accurate histories and other information in order to develop the treatment plan. If the patient minimizes or denies many of the problems, and the family isn't available to set the record straight, then the treatment team is at a terrible disadvantage.

If the patient refuses to sign a release, the treatment team won't be able to contact the family. But that doesn't mean the family can't communicate with the treatment team. It is right and proper for family members to mail or fax detailed information to the therapists so the treatment team can get an accurate picture of the situation.

Case History

Throughout this book, we will use case histories to illustrate our points. We'll begin now by showing how a good multidisciplinary team develops an individualized treatment plan to carry out a full continuum of care to help a patient begin his recovery.

Let's call our twenty-eight-year-old male patient Jack, a man who has been drinking heavily for ten years, has taken a multitude of drugs, and has suffered from anxiety and depression since his preadolescent years. In addition, he has just been in a severe car crash, has a broken leg, and may have sustained a closed-head injury. Two friends of his were seriously injured in the accident.

After medically detoxing the patient, a residential treatment center experienced in dual diagnosis will begin a weeklong assessment process. The various members of the multidisciplinary team will do a variety of tests and interviews with Jack to assess him from every angle. The certified addiction counselor will get a chemical use history, the social worker will get a psychosocial history, the psychologist will do various kinds of testing (such as the MMPI-II, the Minnesota Multiphasic Personality Inventory) and interviewing, the psychiatrist will consult on possible medications, and the spiritual counselor will assess grief, loss, and spiritual considerations. In addition, a recreation therapist will design an exercise plan, a nutritionist will consult on dietary considerations, and the medical team, which has recently completed Jack's detox, will consult on any ongoing medical issues.

Since we are also worried about a possible closed-head injury, we may also call in a neuropsychologist or neurologist to do specialized testing around this issue. This may require a visit to a hospital. If PTSD (post-traumatic stress disorder) becomes more of an issue as treatment progresses, perhaps as a result of the injury to Jack's friends, then a psychologist specializing in this problem may play a greater role in treatment.

In an ideal situation, the members of the multidisciplinary team will meet on a weekly basis to discuss the case. Their initial meeting, after all the assessments have been completed, will be to design Jack's treatment plan. As time goes on, they will start focusing on aftercare issues. Does he need extended care in a residential setting? Can he move to a halfway house and begin working? Can he return home and continue with therapy and AA?

Most treatment centers claim to have a multidisciplinary model, and many are making serious efforts to bridge the gaps among the various disciplines. But if you are one of Jack's parents, how will you know if the team is working as it should? What are the questions to ask?

Presuming Jack has signed the appropriate releases of information so you can talk to the staff, here are some things to consider: First, does the person managing Jack's case call you in a timely manner? This case manager should make contact within one week of his leaving detox. The case manager should also be gathering information from you, an important secondary source of knowledge. After all, Jack may still be minimizing his alcohol and drug use, or he may not want to talk about the anxiety problems that go all the way back to grade school. You will have to make sure that the staff knows what you know.

Next, you should make sure that Jack has been seen by all the individuals mentioned previously and that there has been a group effort to develop his treatment plan. If your conversation with the counselor or case manager leaves you feeling uncertain, ask to speak to the clinical supervisor. Ask this person how the psychologist's and psychiatrist's assessments have been incorporated into the treatment plan. For example, if PTSD has been identified, how will it be treated? Will there be special sessions with a psychologist trained in this area?

When a good multidisciplinary team is working together, an integrated treatment plan will be developed that emphasizes both recovery from addiction and treatment for mental health issues. It is vitally important that Jack starts working through the Twelve Steps (he likely won't go beyond Step Five in a residential setting), but it is equally important that his issues of anxiety and depression are properly addressed. Is medication required? Does it need to be changed because of side effects that are only noticed after a week?

If you aren't comfortable with the answers you are getting from the counselor or case manager who is appointed to communicate with you, don't hesitate to go to a higher authority. It doesn't pay to be aggressive or to badger the clinicians, but it's important to make sure everyone is doing his or her job.

It is also critical that you attend the family program. Every good treatment center offers this component, and you must make time in your schedule to participate. After all, you will still be dealing with Jack six months or six years from now, when the clinicians at the treatment center have left the picture. So you must learn as much as possible during Jack's treatment, both to understand what you can do to help and to understand what you cannot do. There is a balance for families too.

As primary residential treatment is concluded, Jack may be transferred to an extended-care facility, where he will stay for three to six months. Here he will continue to work on PTSD issues, and he will become involved with the local AA community. By the third month, he may be expected to get a part-time job so he can start functioning in society again. All the while, he will be in a controlled environment, and he will be randomly tested for alcohol or drug use. He will continue to work closely with a treatment team, and he will get an AA sponsor to guide him in his recovery. After six months of treatment, he may find that he needs a very low dose of medication to manage his psychiatric symptoms. When he completes extended care, he may choose to live in a sober house with other recovering men for another six months instead of getting an apartment by himself.

In this way, over a period of months, Jack will progress from being an active alcoholic with psychiatric problems to being a self-sufficient individual who is taking charge of his own recovery. The proper continuum of care will bring him from a point of crisis to a stable recovery. From this point onward, he can continue with AA meetings and individual counseling. Like millions of others before him, he can get his life back in a way that's better than it's ever been before.

3

What Hurts? What Helps?

In this chapter, we will cover some of the consequences of co-occurring disorders—fundamental principles about the behaviors of those who are addicted, the patterns of addiction, and how all of it affects family members. These principles are a starting point in the journey of helping and healing. The points we cover apply to the person with the co-occurring disorder and sometimes to family members as well. Addiction is a family disease, with each member needing to address his or her own issues.

What Hurts?

Denial and Stagnation

Denial is a complex process of selective perception that prevents an addict from seeing what is causing her pain. Denial includes and involves the family. In the book *No More Letting Go*, interventionist and author Debra Jay describes addicts as "masters of misdirection." They can perform sleight-of-hand tricks that seem to make entire events, symptoms, and crises disappear. Addicts often blame others for their problems, absolving themselves of responsibility. By blaming others, they are able to convince themselves that what they're doing is okay.

Denial spreads when addicts make loved ones feel as if they are at fault. They may use a diagnosis or a condition, such as an anxiety disorder, as an excuse for dysfunctional behavior.

"Don't you understand? My panic attacks make it impossible for me to hold a job." Some family members want to believe the addict. They feel that the addict needs their undying loyalty and love. Other family members question statements that instinctively don't ring true, but even they, over time, become conditioned to the manipulation. Other family members don't buy the stories for a minute but are at a loss for what to do. Before long, family members begin to question their own sanity. They don't know what to believe about the disease, the addict's behavior, and the potential consequences, and so they choose to believe what makes them feel safest.

Denial stems from a place of wanting to believe that all will be fine or that all will return to how it was before the addiction reared its ugly head. The addict has lied to family members, and now family members must lie to themselves. Confused by their self-deception, family members do not take appropriate action. They may attend to or treat the anxiety while completely overlooking the addiction. The result is that families spend all their energy reacting, or stamping out fires. As soon as one fire is extinguished, another one lights up.

Denial is what keeps sickness active; it is the oxygen feeding the illness. Family members display denial through a chronic state of crisis fueled by an urgency to fix what is wrong. "More money, new car, rescue for the crisis of the day? No problem; we will make it better, but we will not discuss what is really causing it." Family members are held hostage so long, they sometimes suffer from Stockholm syndrome, a condition in which people take on the values and beliefs of the one who holds them captive. Family members begin to believe the propaganda of the disease. The longer they are held captive, the harder it is to break the denial and stagnation. In addition, the unwritten contract is that the loved one will decompensate, or erupt into a rage, if challenged by any alternative reality. The problem is not us or our loved one, but the addiction and the mental illness.

Denial is a huge manifestation of a co-occurring disorder on the part of the patient and the family. As long as there is a lack of dialogue, a lack of action, and a lack of clarity, things cannot and will not change. Breaking denial is the first step toward healing.

Indulging the Addict

Unconditional love is often seen as the key to helping others. While desirable in many instances, if misapplied to an active addict, it can make things much worse. Meeting the needs of injured or sick family members is instinctive and often plays into one basic fear: They will die unless we help them. There's a point where love and support can become more harmful than helpful.

As loved ones get sicker, families often try harder and harder, doing more and fixing more and expecting different results. Logic is lost. We see this as a stress response, a reaction to the helplessness, fear, and trauma experienced by the family. Under stress, family members shift between two extremes: either bending over backward to help or erupting into angry outbursts. Some family members provide mood-altering substances for their loved ones in order to avoid trouble. Similarly, some physicians who mean well but are misguided, manipulated, or incompetent provide addictive substances in an attempt to "fix" specific symptoms in a dual disorder patient.

Family members often provide money, support, and care with the best of intentions, but when the dually diagnosed person is protected from facing serious consequences by well-meaning support, he has no real motivation to change. Isolation, dysfunction, and addiction continue. It is important for the family to create expectations and set conditions for support. This may not be easy to do, especially if our loved one is used to getting his way. The assistance of a professional or the involvement of an interventionist may be needed to change the "contract"—the unspoken, unwritten agreements—in a humane, effective, and healthy way.

Punishing the Addict

Just because unconditional love can make matters worse doesn't mean the opposite strategy will work. Becoming angry, controlling, threatening, judgmental, or harsh are equally ineffective techniques. We have observed patient, loving, and kind families become exhausted and then angry. They change the contract suddenly, taking their loved one to task over minor transgressions. Instead of addressing the larger problems, they blow up over a missed appointment, a dirty car, or a harsh comment. This sudden shift almost always backfires. It fuels shame, confusion, and fear.

Absence of Structure

Families often get manipulated into supporting their loved one in a lifestyle free of responsibilities, accountability, or structure. Whether "working the system" or "working the family," the dual disordered manage to use mental illness or addiction as a means of avoiding the daily structure and responsibility that keep most of us healthy. They are too sick, too anxious, too depressed, or too high to hold down a job, to volunteer, or to go to school. When they avoid responsibility, they lack structure in their lives. This avoidance behavior is not due to laziness or mean-spiritedness. It is simply the nature of the diseases.

The absence of a daily routine allows things to stay the same, and over time, things get worse. Sleep patterns reverse, depression gets worse, and confidence deteriorates. The logic is almost always inverted: "My behavior will change once I feel better." Incidentally, this faulty logic is countered effectively by AA, which stresses action and personal responsibility. Recovery from a co-occurring disorder requires a lot of action on the part of the patient. Recovery programs don't work by themselves, like a magic pill. Rather, as they say in AA: "It works if you work it."

Isolation

Loneliness, isolation, and lack of a personal support system make the addict and family feel worse and tend to amplify negative emotions. Absence of social support increases vulnerability to stress and relapse. We are social creatures; depression, anxiety, and trauma-based disorders, among others, can make people believe that they cannot socialize or function with others. Isolation then becomes a lifestyle, justified by feelings of uniqueness and shame. People suffering from co-occurring disorders tend to stay by themselves or have friends who are usually suffering from similar problems. Once again, the logic is inverted: "I must stay by myself until I feel better." But isolation feeds the illness. The exact same pattern can affect the family. As a loved one becomes more symptomatic, families isolate as well, overwhelmed by pain and confusion.

Too Much Thinking

If those with co-occurring disorders could redirect the energy they spend on unproductive thinking, they would become a major source of creativity and innovation in the world. Those who suffer from addiction and psychological disorders tend to think a lot. Their thinking patterns are intense, often occurring at night, in a chemically altered state, and in isolation. Most often these thoughts are either impractical or not followed by action.

Depressed and anxious individuals are particularly vulnerable to "ruminative thinking," an obsessive activity that is both exhausting and nonproductive. Individuals with bipolar disorder may have flashes of brilliance and creativity, but often what they conjure is not original and doesn't stand the test of daylight. Similarly, marijuana addicts may feel they are brilliant when high, but this notion fades when the effects of the drug have worn off. Those who use hallucinogens can become inspired by perceptions that are trivial in the light of day.

People suffering from addiction and mental health issues tend to skip the planning, preparation, and execution phases of bringing an idea into reality. They often believe that inspiration is enough, so their ideas fall flat, increasing their feelings of despair and hopelessness.

Families can get caught up in the process of overthinking. They listen with intent, try to be encouraging, and simply become confused and exhausted.

Lack of Self-Care

With the exception of steroid abusers and exercise addicts, most individuals with co-occurring disorders have a poor diet and lack physical exercise, amplifying feelings of helplessness, depression, and anxiety. Again, the patient's thinking tends to be self-defeating: "I will start exercising and improve my diet once I feel better." The reality is that once a person starts making these positive changes, she starts to feel better.

Seeking Single Solutions

Seeking quick-and-easy solutions is a characteristic of both psychiatric and addictive disorders. Loved ones may mislead family members into believing that "everything will be okay if I can make this relationship work," or "I will be fine as soon as I find a better apartment with less noise." Focusing on one problem out of context and ignoring the larger problems is a common error, and one that is easy to get swept into.

Addicts also tend to want treatments that work as fast as the drugs they abused. They want the pill, prescribed or illegal, that will make them feel better. Antidepressants start to bring relief fairly quickly, but without ongoing participation in Twelve Step meetings, addictive behaviors tend to reemerge. Both families and those with co-occurring disorders need to be careful not to be seduced by the illusion of single-factor quick-and-easy fixes.

Getting Angry at Your Loved One

It is easy to become angry with a loved one who is active in his addiction or immobilized by a co-occurring condition. In fact, it is almost impossible not to experience anger, but it is important that family members don't allow this natural frustration to dictate their actions. Pure anger does not motivate people to change. It feeds the shame mechanism, adds to feelings of abandonment, and will probably just ignite an angry response in the other person. It can also cloud communication, clarity, and the need for change. It may sound simplistic, but it is more effective to be angry at the disease than at the person.

It is perfectly appropriate to be assertive and clear, however, especially in regard to an agreed-upon treatment or aftercare plan. It helps if family members agree to monitor each other's behavior carefully and seek outside support in the form of Twelve Step groups, professional assistance, and friends.

What Helps?

Accurate Diagnosis

A major problem in diagnosing co-occurring disorders is that the symptoms of various disorders look identical. Within the mental health arena alone, many, many conditions have overlapping symptoms. Deciding which diagnosis is correct can be tricky, even with high-quality testing. The degree of diagnostic precision for many mental health conditions is not as high as it is for common medical problems. There are no blood tests for depression or for bipolar or anxiety disorders (although medical tests do need to be performed because some medical conditions mimic mental health problems). Making things even more complex is that addictive disorders can also mimic mental health disorders. Lingering damage from drugs and alcohol can result in agitation, depression, sleeplessness, and even hypomania. The shortage of natural chemicals can result in what is known as postacute withdrawal, a temporary state of mood and cognitive disruption that in some cases looks identical to a bipolar disorder. In the late 1980s, lithium was sometimes overprescribed for early recovering alcoholics because of this overlap. Conversely, as we discuss in chapter 6, the damage of some of today's addictive drug combinations can result in lasting damage that appears to induce a bipolar disorder.

Diagnosis, which may seem like a simple task in the process of recovery, is actually an art form that requires considerable sophistication and expertise. Having clarity as to which problems are relevant, active, and needing attention can make a huge contribution toward getting better. With co-occurring disorders in particular, one size does not fit all. Accurate and ongoing diagnosis by a multidisciplinary team employing multiple strategies is needed, and individual treatment plans are essential.

Acceptance

There is considerable confusion about the concept of acceptance. In recovery, it means accepting things as they are, not as you wish them to be. When people accept that they have a co-occurring disorder, a process of coming to terms with reality follows. A healthy acceptance means the individual focuses on treatment and on learning how to manage the conditions. *Acceptance* means not being a victim, but taking action; not being in denial, but seeing clearly. A profound reframing occurs: "I am not hopeless, misunderstood, or crazy. I am an addict with an anxiety disorder. I have an illness, and now I will deal with it." More eloquently stated, it is the well-known Serenity Prayer in action:

> *God grant me the serenity*
> *To accept the things I cannot change,*
> *The courage to change the things I can,*
> *And the wisdom to know the difference.*

What are the things I cannot change? The fact that I have a dual disorder. What are the things I can change? The way I deal with that dual disorder and move into recovery. What is wisdom? Not allowing myself to fall into my old ways of thinking, which cause me to think I can control things I can't. Similarly, family members need to come to a point of acceptance. Working on clearer boundaries, developing a more accurate view of the reality of the conditions, and letting go of control, perfection, and blame are key factors for healing. We strongly urge families to participate in Twelve Step meetings and in the family programs offered by most treatment facilities. Clarity and freedom from the debilitating feelings are vital for well-being. Increasing the family's knowledge, accepting the diseases involved, and making correct attributions (not feeling like you caused everything to go wrong) are what facilitate healing. Acceptance frees families to love and frees them from the need to fix or control.

Top Down and Bottom Up

Top-down interventions refer to changes set into motion by the higher parts of the brain such as thought (cognition), self-talk, perception, beliefs, and spiritual beliefs. Top-down interventions include psychological and spiritual interventions. Psychological techniques modify thoughts, which results in changes that affect beliefs, which in turn affect biochemistry and behavior. Spiritual interventions also have a top-down impact. For example, the facilitation of purposeful action, essentially helping others, as included in the Twelfth Step of AA. Top-down changes, whether psychological or spiritual, are powerful and affect all aspects of thought, behavior, and even biology.

Bottom-up interventions refer to the nonthinking aspects of our being: the biological aspects including the primitive, nonthinking parts of our brains. Bottom-up interventions are just the opposite of top down—that is, when biology is impacted by medicine, food, environment, or other physical factors, thinking and beliefs are affected. Changes to nutrition, medication, rate of breathing, aerobic exercise, and sleeping are bottom-up interventions. For example, the use of an antidepressant may alter the biological circuits that feed a fear response to spiders. If that circuit is interrupted, the perception of spiders is likely to change. Bottom-up interventions can have a powerful influence on biology, and this impacts perception, belief, and behavior and may even impact spiritual beliefs.

Structure

One of the most potent factors in any recovery program is a patient's increase in structured activity. Almost all inpatient treatment programs have a rigorous schedule; hours are defined in terms of recreation, group therapy, lectures, and mealtimes. The increased activity empowers clients through required action and gives them less time to isolate and engage in nonproductive thinking. It is simply a reality of human nature: We need structure and routine, at least to a certain extent. Too much time feeds depression and rumination. Structure imposes expectation and shifts the pattern. Family members can find ways to help increase structure after treatment. Ideas for how to do this are usually part of the aftercare plan.

Because most patients have gotten accustomed to staying inactive with family support, changing the rules will likely result in less than full compliance unless there has been adequate preparation. Before changing the status quo, families should plan ahead. Working closely with the appropriate aftercare and program professionals will help patients and families transcend resistance to change.

Effective Confrontation and Support

Good communication is an art form. Family members know that their loved one can manipulate them in ways that sabotage any discussion about the condition or the process of change. Sufferers will have an emotional outburst, have an anxiety attack, threaten suicide, or act out in any way necessary to silence the family member attempting to confront them. The wrong thing to do is to try to shout them down or shame them. We may win a battle, but we will lose the war.

The only effective confrontations are those that are embedded in a loving message. Although this so-called "carefrontation" sounds simple, it is not. Skilled professionals can help family members avoid becoming too harsh or too soft in their discussions with a loved one. Families need to learn how to remain objective, yet supportive. It is often easiest to do this when at least two family members talk to the loved one.

If, for example, a loved one is failing to live up to her aftercare plan by not attending therapy meetings and not taking prescribed medications, it might be appropriate to say the following: "Jane, we all made an agreement in treatment that you would go to your psychologist twice weekly and take Zoloft. I know you haven't refilled your prescription, and you haven't been to a session in more than a week. We agreed on what would happen if you refused to follow the aftercare plan, and I'm willing to enforce that agreement. Do you want to continue living here, or do you want to go to a halfway house? You must make a choice. You either honor your agreements or you move out."

What the family is saying here is that the patient's actions will determine what level of care she needs. If she really can't follow through with her agreement, then she needs a higher level of care, namely the halfway house. The family members are not being punitive, they are merely acknowledging the fact that they aren't able to give her the amount of support she needs. The patient, for her part, must do the hard work necessary to move out of her illness and into recovery. This kind of reality therapy is very effective, even with seriously ill patients. There are no shortcuts.

Social Support

Individuals who have co-occurring disorders tend to suffer from a condition called "terminal uniqueness." As the phrase implies, they believe that they are the only ones who have ever had this series of problems and that no one can possibly understand them or help them. This helps them to "compare out" from others who are in recovery, and thus avoid the hard work of recovery. We are all unique, but the path of addiction is predictable. The addict progresses by finding similarities he has with other recovering people.

Finding new and healthy friends and social support is required not only for addiction recovery but also for psychological disorders. Often these new friends will be found in Twelve Step groups. There are also co-occurring disorder support groups. These meetings are sometimes referred to as Double Trouble meetings. Specific disorders also tend to have support meetings, some of which have Twelve Step foundations and others that focus only on the psychiatric condition. Meaningful relationships with peers will help protect loved ones from engaging in self-deceptive thinking, because recovering friends are able to challenge faulty thinking. This is particularly vital when "primitive" urges take over, whether in the form of fear, depression, or cravings.

A healthy peer can provide the top-down feedback that will interrupt a craving or an impulse, or even a panic response. Having support is vital. As they say in AA, "Your head is like a bad neighborhood. You should never go there alone."

Similarly, families may benefit from extra support. Attending aftercare groups, support groups, and individual and family therapy sessions are all options worthy of serious consideration. It is easy to slide into old patterns of behavior. Adding support systems and outside feedback can protect families from the stresses and uncertainties of dealing with a distressed love one who struggles with co-occurring conditions. When family members take care of themselves, they are better able to take care of their loved one.

Conservative Doses of Medication

Medications can make a vital contribution to recovery and to relapse prevention. Not too many years ago, addiction treatment professionals viewed any psychiatric medication as improper.

People suffering from depression were told that antidepressants were addictive and should not be used by addicts. Others were told that medication blocks emotions and stunts the healing process. This is simply not correct, unless the client is improperly medicated or overmedicated. The lowest dose for best effect is the goal. As we have stated previously, many dual disorders do not require medication or may only require medication for short-term stabilization. On the other hand, some people may require medication on a long-term basis. Medication, if properly managed, can be a major contributor to recovery from both addiction and mental illness.

While even the most optimistic pharmacologists do not envision biological cures for either addiction or the complex spectrum of mental illnesses, many exciting developments are evolving. There are medications available now that—for some patients—reduce cravings for some drugs, interrupt the high from opiates, and possibly decrease the craving for alcohol in problem drinkers. Studies are under way to see if specific mood stabilizers will reduce cocaine urges. Although there are no silver bullets, exciting research efforts currently under way are likely to help considerably. Antiaddiction medicine is in its infancy, but other aspects of treatment will always be required. It should be noted that these medications only offer an additional tool in the patient's recovery program. They do not, under any circumstances, take the place of Twelve Step meetings and ongoing therapy. Medical treatment for specific symptoms is only one factor in a multifactor problem. Co-occurring disorders require multiple strategies and approaches, not just medication.

Decades of psychological research have shown consistently that while medication helps, so does therapy. In fact, nonmedicinal therapies are equally effective for some, but not all, psychological disorders. When medication is required, the best outcome is derived from combining it with therapy. As the case studies in the rest of the book will show, medications often play a crucial role, especially in the beginning of the recovery process.

Medications are helpful, but sometimes overprescribed. Become an informed consumer along with your loved one. Knowledge is power, and plenty of information is available. Be careful, however, of Web-based information. Many Web sites are oriented toward sales, not objective knowledge. See the back of the book for sites we recommend.

Some people tend to either fear medications or overestimate their curative power. We tend to trust psychiatrists who take a minimalist approach: fewest medications, lowest effective dose, and shortest time of use. Some severe conditions may require more aggressive medication and other biological therapies. Remember, too, that for many psychological conditions, medication management can be lifelong, and a blessing.

Be wary of addictive medications, especially sleep and anti-anxiety medications such as benzodiazepines, which appear to help the psychological condition but can fuel the addiction. Natural and herbal additives may be appealing, but their doses are difficult to calculate, and mixed with other medication, they can be disastrous.

Manage the Body

Exercise and diet are important for everyone. For those suffering from co-occurring disorders, a healthy regimen is imperative. Healthy lifestyle changes, such as in diet and exercise, can make a huge difference in terms of mood, perception, and sense of well-being. Exercise tends to restore natural stimulants, such as serotonin, and a whole host of chemicals that elevate mood naturally. Proper nutrition (not simply swallowing vitamin pills) adds to this effect. (Be careful of supplements. Some can have harmful consequences, and some may interfere with prescribed medication.) For those who do not have full-blown genetic or injury-related psychiatric imbalances, nutrition and exercise can be some of the most powerful biological treatments available.

It is important to remember that, for those who suffer from psychological conditions, especially anxiety disorders and depression, additional vigilance in self-care is mandatory. People with normal biology may not be as affected by disruptions in dietary or exercise regimens. For people with co-occurring disorders, even minor lapses can result in a significant mood change. For an in-depth look at this subject, as well as practical advice on diet and exercise for recovering people, see *The Wellness-Recovery Connection* by John Newport, Ph.D.

Positive Outlook

When either or both parts of a dual disorder are active, the patient is likely to have a negative outlook. It just goes with the territory. Recovery requires a change in worldview. A positive outlook and a sense of hope are essential. Hope is powerful medicine. As stated by historian and writer Lewis Mumford, "We can live three weeks without food, three days without water, and, yes, we can even live three minutes without air, but we cannot live without hope."

It has been said by those in AA, "Recovery is easy. You just have to change everything." It is impossible to face this daunting task without hope. For some people, simply attending Twelve Step meetings and seeing the success of other people is a source of great hope.

For others, early recovery is a time to connect or reconnect with core beliefs. Questions of faith and ultimate meaning aren't academic to those who have been devastated by these illnesses. Many patients suffering from co-occurring disorders have had the experience of having a drug as a Higher Power. What will be the guiding influence now? Will it be religious faith or moral values or a personal spirituality? Something must fill the void and provide a motivating force for action.

Once hope is restored, progress is almost inevitable. We cannot continually provide hope for our loved ones, but we need to include it in our thinking and in our language. Superior treatment programs include a focus on the spiritual dimension. Whether the client has well-formed religious beliefs or none at all, she must expend real effort to build the hope necessary for recovery. It is a huge factor and a sustaining force in the quest to transcend dual disorders.

It is instructive to think of Step Two of the AA program, which describes what chronic alcoholics have had to do in order to overcome their illness: "Came to believe that a Power greater than ourselves could restore us to sanity." The Step states that it is only necessary to believe that such a thing is possible. In essence, this is an application of top-down change—hope provides soothing at a psychological and neurological level.

The Four Factors

The healing factors cited on the previous pages can be simplified as four vital factors needed for recovery from co-occurring disorders. These factors apply to the family members as well as to the loved one with a co-occurring disorder.

The first factor is *biology*. Biology refers to all the factors that affect physical well-being. This includes medicine, diet, exercise, and healthy sleeping patterns. Scrupulous self-care provides a stronger foundation for sustained change. It is important that you and your loved one be diligent in following the directions given by treatment professionals. Do not be your own doctor.

The second factor is *psychology*. Psychology includes thoughts, perceptions, and the messages of one's inner voice. Altering thought patterns and perceptions requires considerable work and guidance. Sponsors and clinicians participate in this process. Working the Steps, especially working on acceptance, requires open-mindedness and a willingness to accept new knowledge, thoughts, and perceptions. It requires realism and truthfulness about the nature of the problem and the nature of the solution. Working the Steps facilitates the letting go of self-blame and the illusions of control or omnipotence.

The third factor is *interpersonal*. Interpersonal refers to the support systems used on a daily basis. Recovery from addiction and co-occurring disorders does not occur in isolation. Healthy friends and supports are vital. People in long-term recovery often advise newcomers to "stick with the winners." New attitudes and behaviors require active, healthy supports.

The fourth factor is *spiritual*. Spirituality involves more than religion. You need not be religious in order to have a positive spiritual system. Core beliefs often drive perceptions in an almost automatic way. That is, thoughts, or cognitions, are profoundly impacted by spiritual processes. A spiritual vacuum or a highly negative spirituality can interfere with the effectiveness of the other three factors. A direct dialogue about spirituality, in a non-threatening, nondogmatic manner, can be a potent healing factor for co-occurring psychological issues and is an emphasized area of focus for Twelve Step recovery. Addiction counselors, sponsors, and mental health providers participate in the realm of spiritual change. Spiritual changes refer to the highest level of organizing beliefs and attitudes.

Treatment does work, and recovery has become a reality for many. When we are in the midst of chaos, it is difficult to see how to facilitate change. A well-coordinated, well-timed set of interventions that address all the issues outlined in this chapter will vastly increase the likelihood of success. Formulating an action plan may require the help of professionals and/or an interventionist. We have discussed general principles—what helps and what hurts. In subsequent chapters, we will provide more specific information about disorders and treatment.

While we cannot change the behaviors or attitudes of those who are suffering from co-occurring disorders, we have the power to change how we react to them. Recovery is a process, and we can model that process for our loved ones by reaching out for help in a variety of ways. We can get expert advice, attend support groups, and shop wisely for treatment. We can learn as much as possible about specific psychological conditions and seek accurate diagnoses and comprehensive treatments. We can be patient and persistent—the more complex and severe the co-occurring combinations, the more hope, information, guidance, and support we need. Although we won't know it right away, our positive example of change and growth will help to inspire our troubled loved ones.

4

Anxiety Disorders

I wish it were just butterflies in my stomach. Yeah, my heart would pound, and I'd feel like I couldn't get enough oxygen. But I felt this huge hole right in the center of my being. I had to fill that hole and make it all go away. Jack Daniels and a bit of weed seemed to be my only option. It wasn't about choice—it was survival.

Jason, age 24

"Imagine the oxygen being pulled out of the room. This is how an alcoholic feels when he has cravings." This description is sometimes used to teach nonalcoholics what cravings are like for an alcoholic. For addicts, cravings are more than just desire. For addicts who have a co-occurring anxiety disorder, the intensity is compounded. They feel as if they will die unless they find relief, and using drugs or alcohol seems to be the only thing that helps to alleviate the suffering.

Anxiety is a universal human experience; it is a normal response to a threat. We all know what it feels like to experience dread, to anticipate small or large disasters, and to experience the physical grip of fear. Anxiety and fear, however, are quite different. While fear involves actual danger, anxiety involves anticipated danger, perceived danger, or a sense of dread.

An anxiety disorder can be defined as a condition that involves a state of distress and chronic but fluctuating nervousness that is inappropriately severe for the circumstances. Some anxiety disorders involve panic—intense, distressing, short-lived surges in heart rate, tingling, dizziness, shortness of breath, and feelings of impending death.

Anxiety disorders are quite common; about 16 percent of the American population has an anxiety disorder in one form or another. There are many types of anxiety disorders; the specific label, or diagnosis, is determined by the blend of several factors, including types of triggers, duration of symptoms, and intensity of symptoms. All anxiety disorders have a common feature: They are exaggerated responses to natural circumstances.

Biological and Cognitive Aspects

A real threat and a perceived threat produce the same biological changes in the body. When the biology of fear (real or perceived) kicks in, the heart races, blood pressure increases, and hormones start pumping. Blood is able to clot more quickly, and more energy is instantly available to the muscles. These are hardwired natural and adaptive responses to danger that make us stronger, faster, more alert, and ready for "fight or flight." When we are presented with an actual threat, feeling fear can save our lives. When danger is not truly present, and we are feeling anxiety, we put our bodies in a high-stress mode unnecessarily and for long periods of time. This causes changes in stress hormone levels and, in many instances, actual changes in brain biology.

With fear, or actual danger, the changes to our bodies are triggered initially by our senses. A long-standing debate has occurred over whether fear is automatic or the result of our recognizing and thinking about what could cause us harm. In other words, do we experience fear after we see the bear, or do we experience fear before we recognize it is a bear? Modern technology has given us an answer: We experience fear before we even know it's a bear. Saving precious nanoseconds, this rapid response permits us to have a surge in biological functions that gets us moving, even before we know exactly what the threat is.

With anxiety, there is an absence of an actual external threat, and the changes to our bodies are triggered by our cognitions, or thoughts. We talk ourselves into believing the worst possible scenario. How the mind interprets and perceives events, what we choose to think about, our perception of events, our memory, and our self-talk are vital components of anxiety disorders. The difference between normal anxiety and an anxiety disorder depends upon how often we anticipate dread and how long the effects linger. We all experience temporary states of anxiety, but someone with an anxiety disorder may deal with the thoughts and effects of anxiety almost full time, even during sleep. How we think is a huge factor in whether we succumb to or master fear. Our thinking and our beliefs, even in the absence of an actual threat, affect our biological reactions and emotional states. All of us are capable of convincing our bodies to go into fight-or-flight mode, and people who have an anxiety disorder do this on a regular basis.

Why do some people experience normal anxiety and others experience an anxiety attack? Although what and how we think are contributing factors, an anxiety disorder isn't just in a person's head. Research has shown that it's also in the genes. Anxiety disorders do run in families. For example, even when twins are reared separately, the disorder is likely to manifest itself in both. If your Aunt Mary suffered from an anxiety disorder, you may be at higher than average risk for this condition. It is now believed that the genes that increase the likelihood of anxiety disorders are similar to the genes for depression. Future research will likely clarify how large a role genetics plays in each of these disorders and in the combination of both. As with so many questions involving behavior and genetics, it is likely that environment, conditioning, and other factors are involved in complex interactions that vary from individual to individual.

Symptoms

Symptoms of anxiety can be seen in a normal anxiety response, such as when a young person starts to perspire before her first big job interview, believing she is not qualified for the position. In a maladaptive anxiety response, she is afraid to leave her home to go to the interview, thinking she's doomed never to find a job because she believes no one likes her.

People with anxiety disorders experience fear or panic more often and to a greater degree than most people. The experience of anxiety and its progression into an anxiety attack is powerful and can be difficult to manage. During an anxiety attack, a person feels a loss of control of body and mind. Anxiety attacks can include chest pain, feelings of numbness, shortness of breath, a sense of impending death, and feelings of insanity. Anxiety disorders are associated with a high suicide rate, addictive disorders, and other psychiatric problems, including depression.

Those who suffer from anxiety disorders tend to be more isolated. They may avoid social situations or crowds. The fear of having an episode can interrupt the building of intimate supports and friendships or stifle the willingness to explore new avenues for meeting others. Fear of attachment can be another consequence. The attachments they do make may be superficial, and dating may cease. For those already attached, the shame of disclosing anxiety symptoms can create distance in what was once a close relationship.

Anxiety disorders have a common consequence referred to as "a sense of foreshortened future." People with anxiety disorders tend to have a spiritual perspective that nothing is safe and nothing will ever be safe. They do not trust in a Higher Power and see themselves as helpless, hopeless, and abandoned. This spiritual consequence increases with the severity of the anxiety disorder. A mild phobic may not have a spiritual crisis, but someone who has a very pervasive and intense anxiety disorder may lose all hope and may then be at higher risk for suicidal ideation.

The intense symptoms that a person feels during an anxiety attack may be overwhelming, and trying to reason with somebody experiencing an anxiety attack is not likely to help. The anxiety takes possession of the person and feels life threatening, even when the person knows better logically. The desperation is intense—it feels as if survival is in jeopardy, and it demands resolution. The person having the attack thinks, *Just do something to make it stop!* For some people, making it stop translates into using chemicals, or self-medicating. The result is a conditioned response: The person avoids what sets off the anxiety or panic attack and relies on chemicals for instant relief.

Not all symptoms that look like anxiety disorders are the result of an anxiety disorder. Some medical conditions, including diabetes, hypoglycemia, and certain cardiovascular conditions, produce similar symptoms. A good medical workup should always be a part of any diagnostic evaluation.

Types of Anxiety Disorders

Types of anxiety disorders include the following:

+ *Generalized anxiety disorder* is a condition lasting six months or longer and involves daily worry and nervousness about a wide range of events and circumstances. Symptoms include ongoing muscle tension, sleeplessness, fatigue, and poor concentration.
+ *Panic disorder* is a condition characterized by frequent, sometimes random panic attacks that occur without an identifiable trigger. Panic attacks can happen with any anxiety disorder, but they are defined by an identifiable trigger (e.g., a spider or snake). Symptoms include chest pain, dizziness, fear of dying, tingling, numbness, feelings of unreality, shaking, and shortness of breath.
+ *Agoraphobia* is a response to or avoidance of being trapped in places without being able to escape easily if panic occurs. Crowded social settings, including supermarkets, malls, and movie theaters, can set off a panic or avoidance response. Some agoraphobics become housebound. A similar diagnosis is a social phobia, or social anxiety disorder. This condition involves a dread of social performance or a fear of being seen as anxious.

+ *Specific phobias* are irrational fears of specific objects or situations. These include acrophobia (fear of heights), zoophobia (fear of animals), and triskaidekaphobia (fear of the number thirteen). The most common phobia is glossophobia, a fear of public speaking.
+ *Acute stress disorder* is a short-term response to a terrifying event. Symptoms last for up to four weeks and can include emotional numbing, recall and memory problems, and symptoms of panic.
+ *Obsessive-compulsive disorder* is characterized by the presence of recurring, unwanted, and intrusive ideas, images, or impulses that may be dreadful to the person experiencing them. There is also an intense urge to do something that will relieve the discomfort.
+ *Adjustment disorder* is a reaction to a loss or a stressful event that lasts six months or less.
+ *Post-traumatic stress disorder* is a reaction to a loss or stressful event that lasts longer than six months. See chapter 9 for an in-depth description.
+ *Substance-induced anxiety disorder* is an anxiety condition caused by the use of mood-altering chemicals. Individuals who use stimulants and hallucinogens are particularly vulnerable. Most often, symptoms disappear after detox. In some instances, the chemicals create long-lasting or permanent symptoms.

Dietary Factors

Even though diet alone rarely causes an anxiety disorder, caffeine and sugar can play a powerful role. In some instances, they are key contributors to anxiety disorders. Dr. Boriskin's very first patient sought treatment for what looked like an anxiety disorder. The young woman had a fear of driving on ice, a real problem for someone who lived in the Midwest. During the intake, the patient was drinking a cup of coffee. Dr. Boriskin asked her about her coffee consumption. Her casual response was that she routinely drank four pots of coffee per day, her coffee pot capacity being ten cups. A simple change in diet resulted in her symptoms disappearing.

Although it is uncommon that excessive caffeine alone will cause an anxiety disorder, it is well known that caffeine consumption will exacerbate an existing anxiety disorder. In some instances, recovering individuals begin drinking coffee in excess at Twelve Step meetings and in other settings. A few added shots of espresso have triggered profound anxiety and relapses in more than a few patients. It may sound simple, but people suffering from an anxiety disorder, especially those who have a co-occurring addictive disorder, should eliminate or reduce caffeine consumption as part of their recovery plan.

Similarly, sugar consumption, especially for those who are hypoglycemic, can set off anxiety symptoms, also increasing the risk for addiction relapse. The sugar "high" that follows an overproduction of insulin is mood changing and often anxiety inducing. Sugar is not the only culprit. Quickly metabolizing carbohydrates, such as white rice, potatoes, and processed flour products, can spike blood sugar levels, resulting in heart-pounding symptoms for those who are vulnerable. Carbohydrates with high fiber content, such as whole-grain bread, are absorbed more slowly, and blood sugar won't spike as quickly. Adding fat also slows down absorption, so whole-grain bread with some butter will mediate the sugar more than plain bread. In general, reducing sugar and carbohydrate consumption should be a part of the recovery process.

Disorders That Commonly Co-occur with an Anxiety Disorder

Most individuals who have an anxiety disorder also have additional diagnoses, which include varying types of depression, obsessive thinking, eating disorders, hypochondria, and addiction to alcohol or other drugs. When a patient has more than two psychiatric disorders, it is often referred to as a mixed diagnosis, or a *blend* of disorders. Although diagnosis may highlight one condition over another, the blend must be treated as a whole. People develop various blends and multiple diagnoses depending upon their environment, genetics, and conditioning.

Depression is often a consequence of or a precursor to an anxiety disorder. The sense of foreshortened future, social isolation, and dread can easily fuel a depression. In addition, thinking, self-talk, and other psychological factors color many aspects of life. It is very common to see anxiety and depression together. Several serotonin receptor sites overlap with depression and anxiety. This is why several antidepressant medications—selective serotonin reuptake inhibitors (SSRIs), including Zoloft and Paxil—are often helpful with anxiety disorders.

It's not uncommon for individuals who suffer from one form of anxiety disorder, such as generalized anxiety disorder, to simultaneously suffer from another type of anxiety disorder, such as obsessive-compulsive disorder. People who are anxious are typically more vulnerable to obsessive thinking in general. They obsess with dread about things that can go wrong, feeding the biological mechanisms of fear. Anxiety reinforces obsessions. The sufferer, for example, believes that if he doesn't thoroughly wash his hands each time he touches a countertop, he will experience some disastrous consequence. Fear and thought feed off each other, potentially exacerbating both conditions. In some instances, people turn to obsessive behaviors to manage their fear. Some people count or use objects such as rosary beads to help them manage during times of threat.

Often those who have anxiety disorders with obsessive features will exaggerate flaws in themselves, coupling these thoughts with feelings of disaster. When directed at the self, this obsessive thinking can result in a body image disorder called body dysmorphia. Eating disorders are also associated with anxiety and obsessive thinking and can have foundations in irrational levels of fear. Compulsive overeating may involve the use of food to soothe fear, while anorexia might be associated with a fear of consuming food and/or getting fat.

Hypochondria involves an exaggerated fear of becoming ill or dying. The anxiety is highly disproportionate to the actual threat. It is not unusual to see someone who is fearless in one circumstance become terrified by a minor symptom. Any minor change in biology can become a cue for and an obsession associated with a fear of dying. Hypochondria's major fuel is fear of death. Hypochondria is another example of an anxiety disorder that co-occurs with other anxiety disorders. Often it co-occurs with generalized anxiety disorder, obsessive-compulsive disorder, and other features that used to be called "neurotic."

Anxiety disorders are most certainly associated with an increased risk of abusing drugs or alcohol, which can have a soothing effect. With some patients, the path to alcoholism may be set by conditioning or a learned response. For example, a person suffering from an anxiety disorder may learn that he can tolerate social settings if he drinks alcohol. Over time, this experience of anxiety, drinking, and relief teaches, or conditions, him that alcohol is good medicine for his anxiety problem. The next step might be to find reasons to use it more frequently. Perhaps there is an important presentation to be given at work first thing in the morning. Before long, this kind of thinking can lead the person to become dependent on alcohol. Now he has two problems—the initial anxiety disorder and alcoholism.

Many people erroneously believe that if the anxiety disorder is treated, the drinking problem will go away on its own. But if the person has become dependent on alcohol, if he has crossed the line into addiction after years of drinking, he will have two distinct disorders; both must be treated if the patient is to get well.

Alcohol is not the only substance that people with co-occurring disorders gravitate toward. Some will abuse prescribed medications, such as Xanax, Ativan, or Valium (often called alcohol in pill form). Some people find relief in stimulants. Depending upon a person's physiology, a chemical that agitates one person may relax another. Other people will become exposed to prescription pain medication, perhaps for legitimate reasons, and find that it also calms anxiety. Once again, the stage is set for abuse and addiction. Many young people prefer marijuana because of its easy availability and its tendency to slow the user down. The bottom line is that addictions can develop when people rely on chemicals to soothe painful symptoms.

Which Disorder Should Be Treated First?

As noted in chapter 2, a patient's addiction is the first priority, but attention to the anxiety disorder must begin during the addiction treatment process. The patient must be detoxed and treated for substance abuse at the same time that the anxiety disorder and any other co-occurring mental health issues are addressed. During the first days of treatment, it may be necessary for the anxiety disorder to be managed with prescribed medications, if only to prevent the patient from leaving treatment. Over time, however, medication may become unnecessary.

Families can play a key role in the initial assessment and treatment process. It is important to provide the treatment team with a thorough history before the patient is admitted. Patients often minimize their substance use so they can continue in their addiction. Similarly, many patients will deny their anxiety disorder so they can fit in with the rest of the treatment population. Family members can give the treatment team an honest picture of the situation, helping to ensure that the most important issues are understood and addressed from the beginning.

How Do We Treat Anxiety Disorders?

Numerous treatments are available for anxiety disorders. Simple anxiety disorders are relatively easy to manage. They respond well to new conditioning and repeated exposure to the cause of anxiety. This is a learning process, involving systematic skill building.

One form of treatment involves imagery and desensitization, or practiced relaxation responses. Many of the newer treatments involve going into the environment that is a source of anxiety with a therapist who facilitates a calm response in the presence of the source of fear.

There are many variants of conditioning techniques. Some rely on breathing, guided imagery, or exposure. Positive self-statements, affirmations, distraction, and actual exposure are among the many tools experts can utilize and teach. Mastering certain skills and confronting circumstances of dread can be empowering and life changing for the person suffering from mild anxiety or phobias.

When the anxiety is more severe, as it usually is with co-occurring disorders, several approaches often need to be integrated into a treatment plan, including medication. One simple, nonaddictive medication is actually a blood pressure pill: propranolol, originally used in treating the fear of public speaking. Some of the selective serotonin reuptake inhibitors (SSRIs), such as Paxil and Zoloft, are effective in helping many, but not all, individuals who suffer from anxiety disorders. A new class of antidepressants that works on both the serotonin circuit and the norepinephrine circuit also appears to be effective.

These medications, used alone, will not likely help those with more severe anxiety disorders, but when coupled with therapy, success rates go up. The most difficult cases sometimes require additional residential treatment and support in order to help patients achieve a level of confidence before venturing back out into the world.

Propranolol can be used short term and is nonaddictive. Antidepressants, although not addictive, take longer to become effective and may cause some complications or side effects. The antidepressants help many, but not all, and must be used with careful guidance. In many instances, they can be discontinued once symptom relief is securely established. It should also be noted that the tricyclics, an older class of antidepressants, are also helpful with anxiety. Imipramine, in particular, has been well researched. It is nonaddictive, but it can have side effects that include weight gain, blood pressure elevation, and heart rhythm idiosyncrasies. Although effective, tricyclics must be used with careful guidance and monitoring.

Another class of old-style antidepressants effective with anxiety is the MAO inhibitors. They can conflict with certain foods and other medications, but they are tried when other options fail. Although nonaddictive, they do have side effects worthy of careful consideration.

The class of medication known as anxiolytics, or antianxiety medications, can be safe and effective for nonaddicts. These medications, including Xanax, Klonopin, Librium, Valium, and Ativan, have high potential for abuse and can be addictive. Widely used a few decades ago, these medications are now prescribed with much greater caution due to their addictive qualities. Those who become addicted face an excruciating detox, often described as more difficult than heroin detox. Withdrawal symptoms may linger as long as six months. Anxiolytics, or antianxiety medications, should not be used by those who are vulnerable to addiction or have a history of addiction.

It is important for those who have or may have an addictive disorder to be aware that many of the currently prescribed sleep medications are chemical cousins of the anxiolytics and are therefore addictive. One new addition is a sleep medication that affects melatonin, a hormone that appears to regulate the sleep cycle. Although loss of sleep is a common problem with anxiety disorders, the majority of sleep medications are addictive. There are some nonaddictive options, and an addiction-savvy psychiatrist can provide alternatives.

With very severe anxiety, antipsychotic medication is some-times prescribed. It is helpful in slowing down intrusive thoughts and subsequent biological reactions, and it is not addictive. Because the use of antipsychotics involves potentially serious side effects, these must be used as a last resort and for as short a time as possible.

If the patient is dually diagnosed, treatments for anxiety must be provided during periods of abstinence from mood-altering chemicals. An active addiction will disrupt any technique or combination of techniques designed to treat the anxiety disorder.

Group therapies tend to speed up the healing process for an addictive disorder, and those with anxiety disorders might benefit from the addition of individual therapy with a focus on skill building. Individualized treatment plans and flexible approaches are vital. For those who suffer from anxiety disorders with a co-occurring addictive disorder, building hope, developing coping skills, and being involved in a Twelve Step program is the most effective combination. A perfect outcome is not a requisite or an expectation. Many people continue to struggle with one or more phobias while maintaining sobriety. They create realistic expectations, and, although not symptom free, they learn to cope. Addressing expectations of perfection, or black-and-white thinking, can be a critical factor in dealing with anxiety as well as other co-occurring disorders.

Summary

An anxiety disorder can result in tremendous disruption to mind, body, and spirit. Untreated, an anxiety disorder can override logic, limit options, change relationships, and co-occur with an addiction. Some anxiety disorders precede the addiction, whereas others develop after the onset of the addiction. The intense and primitive fear reactions set off by an anxiety or panic disorder can override logic and lead to irrational choices. Those who suffer from severe anxiety disorders avoid anxiety-inducing circumstances, and when anxiety is triggered, they will often seek out methods of instant relief. If they are addiction prone, an addiction or relapse is likely to follow. Anxiety disorders, when properly treated, are manageable. Scrupulous self-care, productivity, and healthy social supports are part of the formula for success. Good treatment providers, inpatient and outpatient, will cover all core factors simultaneously. They will treat the mind, body, and spirit, and they will address social support.

Anxiety disorders range in severity and complexity and are often intertwined with addictive disorders. They may speak different languages—anxiety demanding instant relief while addiction seeks escape or the high. Multiple treatments work for any one of these conditions, but treatments must be combined in a fashion and at a level that meets the severity and complexity of your loved one's disorder. Single solutions to complex problems do not work, nor does the wrong level of care. Accurate diagnosis is vital, family participation in treatment is extremely helpful, and a multilevel treatment plan that takes into account the biological, psychological, interpersonal, and spiritual aspects of the conditions can result in excellent outcomes. As with all co-occurring disorders, the more severe the symptoms, the greater the level of care needed. The good news is that there are resources that work.

Case History

Jeff Jay recently conducted an intervention that demonstrates the difficulties of trying to help an addict who is also suffering from an anxiety disorder. Here is the experience in Jeff's own words.

> I was first contacted by Peter's family because his life was disintegrating. A lawyer living in San Diego, he was suffering from alcoholism, anxiety, and depression. He was able to function marginally at his job, but his marriage was collapsing, and his parents were worried that there might be more severe problems. Peter often locked himself up in his firm's law library at night, accomplishing nothing and drinking by himself. He refused to admit to having any problem, and he used his skill as a lawyer to deny the desperation that was obvious to everyone.

Peter's misery and isolation caused his young wife and family to worry that he might harm or kill himself.

I worked with Peter's family and friends to prepare for an intervention. Our discussion of Peter's anxiety and depression was low-key and did not include any worries about suicide (these were revealed to me later). The family's story, even under close questioning, didn't suggest any serious problems. Instead, Peter's case sounded like many I had dealt with previously: an all-too-common mix of alcoholism and anxiety sitting on a bed of depression.

When intervention day arrived, however, we were confronted with an unusual situation. Although we were using a very loving and nonconfrontational approach in the intervention, Peter began shaking uncontrollably and speaking in rapid and pressured phrases. He ran out of the house, pushing his mother and sister away violently, and drove off in his car, saying he had urgent business. Peter had experienced a panic attack and was unable to participate. But before he drove away, I was able to extract a promise from him to meet again later that day.

Acting through intermediaries, I advised Peter to take one or two of the sedatives prescribed by his doctor before coming to the intervention, which was not inappropriate given his level of discomfort. The team assembled at the appointed time and proceeded to read their loving and insightful letters aloud to Peter. Although he was deeply moved and seemed ready to change, Peter refused to accept inpatient treatment. He couldn't give any particular reason for refusing help, but he wouldn't give an inch. We tried to negotiate with him, running through almost every trick in the book. Unfortunately, our efforts came to a standstill because Peter had no real objections. He just refused to get any kind of help.

After more than two hours and a break in the process, I realized that the panic disorder was the number-one stumbling block. Peter could not articulate this problem, nor could he even acknowledge that he had such an issue, but I sensed that he couldn't leave his comfortable routine. He simply couldn't imagine himself leaving his home, his pills, and his alcohol. Indeed, we later found out that Peter had seriously considered suicide over the preceding two weeks rather than asking for help or acknowledging his problems.

The key to the intervention was the fact that Peter was suffering from a severe anxiety disorder and was willing to take any other avenue, including suicide, rather than do something that would increase his anxiety. You might say that he was scared to death. Thus, it was necessary to convince him that he would not be allowed to experience any adverse symptoms if he agreed to go to treatment. In other words, I told him, he would be medically managed by the treatment professionals.

"Let me explain that in two words," I said to Peter. "Good drugs." He was listening. "If you agree to go to treatment, I will make sure that the staff is prepared to treat you from the first moment you arrive, and you will be given the appropriate medicine. Oh, and there's no reason to quit drinking before you go to treatment. If you'd like a drink or two on the plane, that's okay."

Peter relaxed, immediately slumped back on the couch, and within two minutes agreed to go with me to treatment. For him, the fact of his alcoholism and his depression was easy enough to admit. But what he couldn't explain was his crippling anxiety. He dreaded change and felt he would die if his anxiety could not be controlled. Peter didn't think he could handle a strange place. He had worked out a routine in which he could go to work and self-medicate with alcohol and tranquilizers (prescribed by a psychiatrist). He was fairly miserable in his life, but he was convinced that it was the best life he could have. If he was always close to his next drink or pill, he was doing the best that he could.

After a thorough assessment, the multidisciplinary treatment team was able to develop a plan for him with both medical and clinical components. Thus, he was quickly weaned off sedatives and placed on appropriate anxiety medication. The new medication was effective because alcohol was no longer in his system.

Peter was able to complete his inpatient treatment plan over a period of thirty-one days and return to his wife and his job. He joined Alcoholics Anonymous and made new friends. He fired his old psychiatrist and psychologist, neither of whom had considered the fact that he was drinking while using sedatives, and instead began working with a new team recommended by the treatment center. Not surprisingly, his depression quickly lifted as his recovery progressed because the depression was based on the external factors of his life (an exogenous depression). Once he was in recovery from alcoholism and once his anxiety was adequately managed, his depression was alleviated.

The initial thrust of the intervention did not address Peter's needs (as he saw them), and so it was ineffective. But once the strategy was adjusted to meet Peter's needs as Peter saw them, the intervention succeeded.

If recovery from addiction and anxiety disorders were simply a matter of making better choices or rational decisions, treatment would not be necessary. And while it's true that better choices and rational decisions are the hallmarks of recovery, they are not to be expected of the practicing addict. Similarly, an anxiety disorder, when experienced as profound panic, shuts off logic. The goal of good treatment is to deal with the reality of addiction and to help your loved one manage anxiety without the use of addictive substances.

5

Depression

Most times it comes on slowly, like a thief stealing in the night. I feel empty, hopeless, and oh, so alone. Nobody can make me feel better, and all those platitudes just piss me off. Why doesn't anyone understand I am not choosing to be depressed—it just happens? When I'm really lost, I cannot stop thinking about all my mistakes and everything I did wrong. I can't get out of my own way, and even the simple things like washing my hair are impossible. I used to try drinking away those feelings, but then I found cocaine, and later crack cocaine. The one time I tried crystal meth, I felt happiness like never before. Even though I know better, it still feels like these are my only friends.

Sandra, age 41

Spencer Tracy had it. So did Ernest Hemingway. Winston Churchill called it "the black dog." In a given year, about 3 percent of all Americans will experience an episode of clinical, or severe, depression. Depression is sometimes easy to treat and other times stubbornly destructive. It is frequently either missed, overdiagnosed, or incompletely treated. It affects men and women from all walks of life; sometimes it's associated with specific disappointments; other times it develops with no apparent reason. Depression covers a wide range—it can be mild and temporary, or it can be recurrent, disabling, and deadly.

Thanks to saturation advertising, most people are familiar with the biological aspects of depression. The simple biological solution is compelling: Take a pill and the problem will be fixed. A large number of clinically depressed people respond to these medications; they are effective and they save lives. Depression, however, is a complex condition that has many possible causes and treatments.

Writers, artists, and philosophers have struggled with the meanings and origins of depression. Writer Susan Sontag said, "Depression is melancholy minus its charms." Olympian Penelope Sweet is quoted as saying, "Depression is nourished by a lifetime of ungrieved and unforgiven hurts." Existential psychologist Dr. Rollo May stated, "Depression is the inability to construct a future." Andrew Solomon, author of *The Noonday Demon: An Atlas of Depression*, offers several descriptions of depression, including "grief out of proportion to circumstance" and "a condition that is unimaginable to anyone who has not known it." The classic psychoanalytic teaching is that depression is anger turned inward. While this definition is still useful, it is far from complete. Analytically based talk therapy requires expressing what fuels our anger. This approach maintains that working out the emotion and reinterpreting our anger is what will resolve depression. While the analytic style of talk therapy alone works with some people some of the time, depression often defies such elegant simplicity.

So how do we define *depression* from a modern context? First, we must refine our language. Sadness, grief, melancholy, and feeling blue are universal experiences—these terms describe normal pain and loss. Clinical depression is persistent, it disrupts lives, and it includes symptoms such as lack of energy, feelings of sadness, poor concentration, rapid weight gain or loss, feelings of hopelessness, brooding, too much or too little sleep, self-deprecation, and sometimes suicidal ideation. To keep it simple, when we speak of depression in this chapter, we are referring to diagnosable clinical depression, not the transitory state of feeling bad for a few days or weeks. Duration as well as intensity of sadness are factors in determining which type of depression a person suffers from and how severe it is.

Some depressions are obvious to outside observers, and many depressions are embedded in complex mood disturbances or acting-out behaviors. Some very depressed individuals appear defiant, not depressed. Sometimes what appears to be depression is another condition (often medical) and, conversely, what appears to be another disturbance is actually an offshoot of an underlying or co-occurring depression.

Types of Depression

We can look at depression in terms of the two major types: endogenous (internal) and exogenous (environmental). Some researchers have challenged this distinction because the differences between biological and environmental factors can be difficult to separate.

Endogenous Depression

An endogenous depression is a biological depression that is the direct result of a biological process or a biochemical anomaly. This type of depression is caused by a biochemical shift in the brain. It may be triggered by an external event, but its power and persistence are defined by brain chemistry.

An endogenous depression is almost destined to happen. Many scientists contend that depression is a genetically determined brain disease that may be set off by a traumatic event, a change in environment, a shift in hormones, or for no reason at all other than the genes being ready to deliver their effect. This perspective views depression as a medical condition—something that happens to a person regardless of her willpower or her successes or failures in life. This view removes the stigma and shame and also explains why some people get depressed even when they are surrounded by people who love them and seem to have everything going for them.

There are several variations of endogenous depression. The most common is associated with a serotonin problem. Serotonin is a neurotransmitter, a brain chemical that transmits nerve signals, and shortages of serotonin are associated with the majority of depressions. SSRIs, which include Zoloft, Prozac, Paxil, and other antidepressants, work directly on the biology of depression. They take three or more weeks to start working, and they are helpful to many. It has been estimated that they are helpful to about 70 percent of those who suffer from depression. While they help with the biochemical aspect of depression, recent research has shown that those who have additional forms of therapy fare much better. The 30 percent who do not respond to SSRIs may need more complex medication, other medical interventions, and psychotherapy.

Some endogenous depressions involve another neurotransmitter: norepinephrine. This type of endogenous depression may be treated with Wellbutrin, which affects norepinephrine and dopamine levels. Wellbutrin can be used together with an SSRI. Endogenous depression may also be treated with a selective norepinephrine reuptake inhibitor (SNRI), such as Cymbalta or Effexor. In addition to affecting serotonin, these medicines can affect norepinephrine levels and also help relieve anxiety for some. The development of the SSRIs, and now SNRIs, has been a great help to patients who have not been able to find relief through other means.

Exogenous Depression

An exogenous depression involves outside factors. Exogenous depression is caused by life-changing events or crises such as the loss of a job or the death of a loved one. Sometimes called a reactive depression, situational depression, or an adjustment disorder, exogenous depression revolves around things that happen in the world that we have no control over, that we have a hard time accepting, or that change our lives in a way that is contrary to how we'd like them to be. Events can alter perception, which then affects the brain. How we think and what we experience can alter our brain chemistry; our brains are capable of duplicating the biology of depression.

The event could be a tragic incident that destroys a belief system or takes someone from us. Or it could be when something meaningful in our lives ends, such as working toward a higher degree, training for a marathon, running for office, or moving from a home after fifty years. These events are usually clear and identifiable: "After my son died, my world fell apart, and I couldn't function normally anymore."

Biology may be involved, but an exogenous depression will not occur unless there is an event. Modern research shows that events, positive or negative, will alter brain chemistry, anatomy, and function. The biological, attitudinal, and behavioral changes would not be set into motion without an event of sufficient impact.

Exogenous depressions respond well to psychological therapies and may or may not require medical intervention. Cognitive therapies, grieving, and changes in attitude are the first line of intervention for exogenous depressions. Changes in environment, schedules, surroundings, and other external factors are often vital in recovering from this type of depression. These types of changes will begin to affect brain chemistry in a positive way.

We'll talk more about events and perceptions of those events in chapter 9.

Blurring the Lines

In reality, most depression involves a combination of internal and external factors. Dividing depression into biological (endogenous) and environmental (exogenous) factors can be overly simplistic. Research shows that for almost all types of depression, a combination of medication and psychotherapy is most effective. But not everyone needs both, and many studies contradict each other. Not all endogenous or exogenous depressions respond to or require medicine. There are more natural options.

Dysthymia

Dysthymia is a form of depression that is mild but persistent, often lasting two or more years. Dysthymia used to be called a neurotic depression and is typified by the characters portrayed in classic Woody Allen movies. These individuals have a fairly negative worldview, feel easily discouraged, and almost always feel a low grade of sadness that may not be related to clear, identifiable events or losses. Dysthymia is sometimes considered harder to treat. Medication may or may not be indicated, but lifestyle and attitudinal changes are usually helpful. People with dysthymia tend to have episodes of severe clinical depression. It is not clear if this is a reflection of a biochemical, genetic vulnerability or if the lingering negative view of the world creates a lower threshold of events needed to set off more severe episodes of clinical depression.

Mood Disorder

Depression may be part of a mood disorder involving highs and lows. Sometimes the highs and lows are not that obvious to the casual observer, and the use of mood-altering chemicals makes it even harder to discern. Those who experience depression associated with the bipolar condition are most often dealing with an endogenous type of disorder. Medications such as SSRIs may work for a while, but then tend to stop working relatively soon. In some cases, an SSRI will set off a sudden surge in energy and mood, called a manic episode. We will examine mood disorders, also called bipolar disorders, in greater detail in chapter 6.

Postpartum Depression

The more spectacular but rather rare cases of postpartum depression include a psychotic variant of depression, oftentimes connected to a mood disorder or a schizoaffective disorder. In most instances, a postpartum depression fits the simpler manifestations of depression: onset of sadness, fatigue, tearfulness without reason, and hopelessness. The key consideration is that in most instances of this type of depression, the symptoms did not exist prior to the delivery of the child.

Although more likely to appear with the first child, it occasionally occurs with a subsequent pregnancy. It is believed that postpartum depression involves the endocrine system, the system that manages the hormonal balance integrally connected to so many mood and biological systems. Mild postpartum depressions seem to pass with time or natural interventions, including the return of a normal sleep pattern when the child matures or additional help becomes available. The more moderate versions may respond to antidepressants. Because hormones are involved, finding the right medication may be tricky.

In some cases, a bipolar disorder will appear as a consequence of pregnancy. It may be that the change in hormones during pregnancy is the triggering event for the bipolar illness. It is not clear how and why this occurs, but it reinforces the idea that there is a complex interconnection between hormones, genetics, and events and the onset of a bipolar disorder.

Depression Associated with Age

Adolescents

The hormonal and bodily changes associated with adolescence can set off a variant of depression. For some, the hormonal changes (endogenous) are the key. For others, the changes in appearance and social expectation can result in stress that we would consider exogenous. Acne, for instance, can set off a crisis of insecurity and isolation resulting in depression. Adolescence is a difficult transition from childhood to adulthood. The rapid changes in body, chemistry, role, responsibility, and expectation can set off a mild depression for many and a severe depression for some.

Another important consideration is that adolescents may not

report their symptoms with the clarity of an adult. They may act out, get into fights, withdraw, and not speak. Many of the so-called rebellious, anhedonic youth wearing only black are not simply articulating their individuality. Some are clinically depressed and quite miserable. Not surprisingly, adolescence represents a high-risk time frame for suicidal ideation, attempt, and completion.

Elderly

Depression associated with aging usually occurs after age fifty and is usually expressed through insomnia, agitation, preoccupation with health, and anticipation of the end of life. For women, these symptoms may coincide with menopause. In some cases, depression in the elderly is clearly identified as the beginnings of other diseases or conditions. For example, it is now known that there is a connection between heart disease and depression, although which comes first is not clear. It appears that serotonin, blood flow, and other factors, possibly including infection, play a role in heart disease and the associated depression.

The denial of the inevitability of death can be an exogenous factor, setting off an imbalance for some older adults. For some individuals, having surgery results in a documented depression believed to be a side effect of anesthesia. Whether reactions to anesthesia represent an exogenous variable due to the surgery or whether the anesthesia sets off an endogenous reaction is not yet clear.

Depression Caused by or Associated with Medical Conditions

Cancer, heart disease, diabetes, kidney disease, thyroid dysfunction, various endocrine disorders, anemia, Parkinson's disease, Alzheimer's disease, multiple sclerosis, muscular dystrophy, syphilis, various liver diseases, chronic fatigue syndrome, HIV/AIDS, stroke, epilepsy, brain injury, and Lyme disease are a partial list of the medical conditions that can set off depression symptoms. Sometimes the diseases cause a direct change in brain chemistry, resulting in the depression; other times the condition or diagnosis of a serious disease will set off an exogenous depression. At least thirty medical conditions include depression as one of the presenting symptoms. Treating only the depression may delay treatment for the actual medical condition, and treating only the medical condition ignores the reality that depression, regardless of origin, may need to be treated as well.

Treating Depression

Biological Methods

Antidepressants are the most common biological treatment. There are three main types of antidepressants—tricyclics, SSRIs, and MAO inhibitors. Tricyclics, an older version of antidepressant medication that affects primarily the serotonin levels, can be effective but tend to have fairly serious side effects, including possible consequences for blood pressure and heart rhythm. (One tricyclic tends to induce fatigue when first consumed, and it is commonly used as a sleep medication for addicts.) The most commonly used antidepressants are the SSRIs. These medications are highly effective and have fewer and generally milder side effects than the tricyclics. Some individuals respond well to one specific SSRI yet do poorly with another. Patience is often required until the correct medication is identified and has an opportunity to work. A third class of antidepressants is the MAO inhibitors. These medications are used with a minority of depressed individuals who do not respond to the other medications. Individuals who take MAO inhibitors must avoid specific foods and medications, including SSRIs.

For individuals in recovery who have been abstinent and depression free for a year or more, there is a great temptation to cease taking antidepressant medications. This is ill advised unless they are working closely with a good psychiatrist. Sudden discontinuation of an SSRI can result in SSRI discontinuation syndrome, which, after a couple of days, can make patients feel disoriented, depressed, agitated, dizzy, nauseated, irritable, and even suicidal. Some individuals feel flulike symptoms, many lose sleep, and others feel as if they are losing their minds. Discontinuation syndrome can make people feel much worse than they originally did and can increase vulnerability for relapse. Even if patients slowly and carefully decrease their medication and avoid this syndrome, for some, the symptoms of depression will come back within three to six weeks. The patient may find that he no longer needs the SSRI, but the decision to discontinue a medication should never be made in isolation and without careful feedback from qualified providers.

One final note about antidepressants: Some sponsors or specific recovery groups will insist that any mood-altering substance cannot be used in recovery. It's important to understand that SSRIs and similar medications are not addictive, even though we now know there may be a withdrawal phenomenon. The presence or absence of withdrawal does not alone define an addictive substance. A depression-managing medication should not be discontinued without the guidance of a qualified professional. Not all depression requires medication, but making the decision to modify or discontinue a medication is an extremely important one that should be done with clear, competent professional guidance.

Another biological treatment for severe depression is electroconvulsive therapy (ECT). This is most often reserved as a treatment of last resort. It is not as cruel or as dramatic as portrayed in Hollywood classics, but it can result in short-term and in some cases long-term memory damage or disruption. Although it sounds primitive, the method does provide symptom relief. It is not a cure, however, and it often requires repetition. Even today, nobody knows exactly why it works. ECT is not used as often as it was in the past because the newer antidepressants work so well for so many.

Several new biological treatments show considerable promise. Vagus nerve stimulation (VNS) appears to have efficacy for some treatment-resistant depressions and is far less intrusive than ECT. With VNS, the body's vagus nerve, located in the neck and extending into the abdomen, receives regulated electrical pulses via a pacemaker-type device implanted in the chest. After surgery, the psychiatrist works with the patient regulating the device until the frequency of stimulation has the desired effect. Although not effective for everyone, the stimulation of the vagus nerve appears to release helpful neurotransmitters for this population of treatment-resistant patients. This surgery has recently been approved for the treatment of resistant depressions and will likely become more common. The surgery is fairly simple and rapid, most often requiring only twilight or conscious anesthesia, but implanting the vagus nerve electrode can be tricky because the surgeon is actually wrapping an electrode around a nerve. Although promising, this is a new technique that may or may not live up to preliminary expectation.

A biological treatment for severe depression that is under development is called transcranial magnetic stimulation (TMS). A magnetic pulse is directed from powerful external magnets to specific areas of the brain, stimulating nerve activity. Neither surgery nor the use of electrodes is required. Doctors utilize a targeted and rapidly changing magnetic field that induces a kind of ripple effect, resulting in increased brain activity to a defined brain area. This highly specific, less intrusive technique may replace ECT. What is particularly exciting in terms of future development is the targeting of specific brain sites for stimulation based upon diagnostic scanning. This method, although promising, is still in the investigational stage.

Natural Biological Methods

Natural methods of biological treatment for depression include aerobic exercise and dietary changes. Sufficient aerobic activity includes daily walking, biking, or swimming—essentially any sustained activity that healthfully increases heart rate. Dietary changes help patients regulate sugar metabolism and help them lose or, in some instances, gain a few pounds. Reducing consumption of carbohydrates and refined sugar and flour and increasing consumption of omega-3 fish oil are healthy dietary changes. Improving health can be incredibly effective if a patient sticks to the changes. Often a therapist can be vital in providing the accountability and momentum needed to put these changes into motion. Aerobic exercise, although not a panacea, stimulates endorphins, increases dopamine, and positively affects the flow of available serotonin. Aerobic exercise can help many individuals manage their depression without medication. Whether a primary or secondary intervention, or even when medication is utilized, increased exercise and nutrients make most people feel better. The usual medical clearances should be obtained before exercise programs are begun.

Psychological Methods

The most rigorously researched and effective form of psychotherapy involves cognitive-behavioral therapy (CBT). Dealing with current and practical aspects of perception, behavior, and decision making with a here-and-now focus, cognitive therapy has been shown to be as effective as medication. Even though we are dealing with a condition that involves solid biochemical and neurobiological features, the evidence is clear that psychological intervention is as powerful as medication. This reinforces current thinking that the lines between biology and psychology are not all that rigid. It also shows that mind affects body—something that has been assumed in Western medicine but has not been clearly understood. Finally, it also shows why top-down interventions, specifically changes in mind-set, thinking, and attitude, can be effective.

CBT is the most widely practiced form of treatment for all types of disorders, but it is not the only model. Most professionals prefer this approach because it focuses on the practical business at hand: changes in behavior. As such, many cognitive approaches are straightforward, but this type of treatment is still an art form.

The clarity of the clinician, the building of trust, and a multitude of other factors affect outcome. Many other schools of psychotherapy and techniques are as effective as cognitive approaches; do not necessarily judge a provider on the basis of theory or technique ascribed to, but do be certain that there is a clarity of focus on realistic goals and changes in behavior. When dealing with depression, perhaps the biggest initial challenge is to get patients into motion *before* they feel better.

Interpersonal Methods

Breaking the pattern of isolation is a vital part of recovery from depression. There are self-help support groups as well as professionally facilitated support groups for depressed individuals. It may take considerable encouragement, at least at first, to facilitate attendance at support groups. As noted above, the biggest challenge is getting the individual to make changes before she feels better. Gentle persistence and "carefrontation" may be necessary to facilitate participation in groups that would actually make the depression less severe. Simply attending a Twelve Step meeting can have a positive impact upon a depressed individual. Forging a relationship with a sponsor or clinician is a vital step forward in breaking the almost addictive aspects of isolation fueled by an active depression.

Spiritual Methods

The spiritual aspects of Twelve Step recovery also assist in dealing with the spiritual aspects of depression. For many, depression results in a profound spiritual crisis. Rejection of more positive spiritual belief systems or attraction to bleak, negative, or nihilistic beliefs is common when depression is present. Advising individuals to change what they read or what they watch on television or film can interrupt the mantra of negativity. Participation in tai chi, yoga, or other Eastern exercises can benefit both body and spirit. In some instances a dialectical behavioral therapy (DBT) approach is helpful. DBT actively incorporates Eastern

philosophy in a nonreligious manner. The addition of dialecticism (the Eastern philosophy component) can have a positive effect on mood and spirit.

Depression and Addiction

Almost all addicts report some form of depression, but this doesn't
mean they are clinically depressed. Many have clear exogenous
forms of depression. For example, a person may have lost his job,
his family, and his finances because of his addiction. But as with
many exogenous depressions, nonmedical treatments will often
be very effective. In most cases, the process of recovery, including
the completion of a reputable treatment program, rigorous aftercare counseling, and participation in Twelve Step groups, will
help to put the patient's life back together. As the person begins
to see progress as a result of his actions, the depression he initially
reported will lift. So, while good treatment providers are on the
lookout for depression, they should not be too quick to add medication at the first report of a problem.

One of the side effects of prescribing medication too quickly
in the case of an exogenous depression is that it will bring about
so much symptom relief that patients may become complacent
and not work at recovery. Having said that, the co-occurrence of
depression with addiction is significant. Most mood-altering substances provide a temporary boost in mood followed by a lasting,
sometimes profound depression.

Alcohol, for example, tends to reduce anxiety and enhance
a sense of well-being at first. The aftermath, however, tends to
be almost the opposite. While this is a mild phenomenon for
nonalcoholics, it can become a profound part of the cycle for alcoholics. Many alcoholics seek treatment for their depression
before they seek treatment for alcoholism. They don't want to
stop drinking, but they do want to minimize the side effects. As
a result, many untreated alcoholics are taking antidepressants.
Evidence suggests that the antidepressant, when used by an ac-

tive alcoholic, tends to make both conditions worse, not better. The exact mechanism is not clear, but the initial salutary effects of the antidepressant are followed by even more dramatic swings in mood as well as anxiety.

As we move through the spectrum of different drugs, whether cocaine, Ecstasy, or marijuana, the connection between depression and addiction tends to become even more dramatic. The effect of these drugs is to destroy the very mechanisms that produce the neurotransmitters that make us feel good. While using drugs, the user feels euphoria and at the same time damages the mechanism that replenishes the normal source of euphoria. In some cases, the damage is irreversible. Perhaps the most potent destroyer of these mechanisms is methamphetamine. It releases twelve times the normal load of feel-good chemicals, and multiple studies show long-lasting or permanent brain damage in the regenerating mechanisms of the brain after extended use. Methamphetamine seems to destroy health more rapidly than almost any other drug. Brain scans show changes in neurobiological functioning as well as actual loss of brain tissue. Similar results are noted for long-term alcoholics. Even people without a predisposition for depression stand a great risk of becoming depressed if they become addicted to almost any mood-altering substance. Depression is a fairly predictable outcome for many addicts.

If we look at a group of individuals genetically predisposed to depression, they also have a higher risk for addiction, even if there is no family history of addiction. The reason for this is that people who are depressed are more likely to seek out and become dependent on chemicals that provide relief from their depression. The irony, of course, is that they will become more depressed as the addiction disrupts their lives. Treating this population, often referred to as social users or problem drinkers, has been the focus of intense controversy. Some treatment strategies involve "moderation management," a skill-building variant of cognitive-behavioral therapy that teaches abusers to find ways to manage emotions without first reaching for a chemical or a drink. While this appears to be a successful strategy for nonaddicts, it is a potentially dangerous and even deadly option when dealing with actual addiction. Given how hard it is to differentiate abuse from addiction for most providers, let alone family members, we urge extreme caution in considering strategies that are not abstinence based. We can never really be certain if our loved one is providing accurate information, is utilizing classic denial, or has actually become addicted. There is little or no risk in an abstinence-based approach and grave risk in moderation management. It's better to err in the direction of overdiagnosing and overtreating what appears to be an ambiguous addiction linked with a self-medicating depression.

The Role of the Family

When a family member suffers from clinical depression, intense emotions are often generated. Feelings of helplessness, confusion, and anger are common. There is no single strategy we can recommend, but we can caution you against some common errors.

Do not engage in endless discussions on the "meaning of life" and the hopelessness articulated by a depressed person. It's difficult to reason with someone suffering from severe depression.

Do not communicate anger to your depressed loved one. What appears to be laziness or unwillingness to change is a function of the depression, not defiance or lack of will.

Do not buy into the "leave me alone and it will all be better" demand. In many instances, letting individuals sort out their own confusion and waiting for things to improve is the right idea. However, with a severe depression, it may be necessary to impose some healthful expectations.

Do not buy into the illusion of "single solutions." Many addicts and depressed individuals are drawn toward black-and-white, all-or-nothing solutions. Recovery from depression, especially with a co-occurring addiction, requires multiple changes—in behavior, lifestyle, routine, beliefs, and support systems. Here are some positive things that you can do, but again, coordinate and time specific ideas with the professionals who are working with you:

+ Focus on a day at a time. The shorter-term focus is helpful with addiction, and it is particularly helpful with depression. Small, achievable daily goals, not large, esoteric ones, can break a pattern. Do not insist, for example, that one's entire living space be cleaned in a day, but start with a drawer or a closet. Be sure the depressed person participates.

+ Encourage greater structure: regular sleep and waking patterns, scheduled meals, and exercise all help with depression.

+ When considering treatment, use a multiprovider, multi-issue approach. Do not rely on medicine alone, for example.

+ Addiction recovery and abstinence are imperative. Depression and addiction feed off one another. Both problems must be addressed, and using always makes things worse.

Family involvement can be extremely helpful, but it may be difficult to keep your emotional and cognitive balance. Engage the necessary support so that you can provide constructive, loving, and effective input. A loved one's depression can be contagious, so families need to get support as well. Family members' clarity and health are perhaps their best contributions. Finally, be aware that a loved one's progress or failure in treatment is in most instances not a reflection of her parents' direct effort. Parents are important but not omnipotent.

Summary

Depression is a complex condition that affects people in powerful and profound ways. There are many types of depression and many causative factors. Addiction is a common co-occurring condition and frequently requires additional specialization and higher levels of care. As with all co-occurring disorders, a multilevel treatment strategy with multiple providers is recommended. It is imperative that both the addiction and the depression be treated simultaneously. Depression affects thinking, logic, and behavior. It is not laziness or displaced willpower. Families need to learn about both conditions, and they must manage their reactions as well. There are no single, simple solutions to most cases, so patience, persistence, and accurate diagnosis are imperative. Insist on the right providers, the correct level of care, and an emphasis on lifestyle and behavioral change. Depression and addiction are both treatable conditions. The resources today are far superior to those just a few decades ago, and with improving diagnostic technology, biochemical approaches, and novel techniques, things are looking better and better.

Case History

Margaret had been through inpatient treatment for alcoholism twice and didn't believe in the process. After her first treatment, at age thirty-one, she achieved almost three months of sobriety, but then started drinking again. After her second treatment, at age thirty-three, she relapsed almost immediately and had been drinking steadily since. At this time, she was thirty-seven.

Until recently, Margaret had been a fairly functional alcoholic, holding down a teaching job and maintaining her own apartment. However, her circle of friends was small, and she hadn't been able to maintain a long-term relationship with a significant other. She was usually attracted to men who were heavy drinkers, and the results were predictable.

Margaret had not been assessed for depression at the first two treatment centers, and she had received no appropriate attention in that area. She blamed her counselors, AA, and herself, in turn, for her treatment failures.

Margaret finally lost her teaching job because she took too many unexplained sick days. She was either hungover or simply unable to get out of bed. She informed her family that she was going to move in with a friend far away and start over. The friend was a waitress in a bar, and Margaret's family was naturally worried.

The family contacted an interventionist (Jeff Jay) and began the planning process for a structured family intervention and a third treatment. In gathering a family history, Jeff soon realized that Margaret was suffering from depression. First, there was a family history of depression, which had long been swept under the rug. Her uncle had committed suicide almost twenty years ago, without warning, and two of her aunts had debilitating bouts of depression at different times. Second, many of Margaret's sick days couldn't be explained by hangovers. She had quit drinking on her own from time to time, but she still didn't always get to work. Third, she had confided in a friend, Sarah, who was part of the intervention team, that she had thought about suicide. Her parents were horrified to hear Sarah say that Margaret admired the uncle who had "taken matters into his own hands."

After gathering this detailed history, the intervention team determined that Margaret should go to a treatment center that specialized in dual diagnosis. Here she would receive simultaneous help for both her alcoholism and her depression. The intervention took place just days before Margaret was to move away. Indeed, she was packing her car when the intervention team arrived.

Although her friends and family were afraid that she would violently resist the intervention (as all families are afraid), Margaret agreed to sit down and listen to what everyone had to say. In the end, she agreed to accompany Jeff to the treatment center with few objections. In retrospect, this isn't so surprising, as her plans to move away were nebulous, at best.

A thorough clinical workup at treatment revealed that Margaret had been suffering from depression since her teenage years, even before she began the regular use of alcohol. She was prescribed a common SSRI, and the dosage was regulated during the course of inpatient treatment to minimize side effects.

Although it took a couple of weeks for Margaret to feel the full benefits of the medication, her reaction to treatment was vastly different than her first two attempts. She worked closely with her counselors and opened up more in group therapy. Because many other patients there were struggling with co-occurring disorders, she did not feel alone or different. Her attitude toward treatment and recovery soon became very positive.

After primary treatment, Margaret agreed to the recommendations of the treatment team and moved into a women's halfway house in a nearby city. This gave her the support necessary to follow her aftercare plan and solidify her recovery. For Margaret, aftercare included continuing work with a psychologist and psychiatrist to address her depression. After a number of months, the dosage of her medication was decreased to a very low level.

She also started benefiting a great deal from Twelve Step meetings. Instead of separating herself from others—focusing on how she was unique and thus didn't belong with them—she started identifying with them. Soon, she started helping new members who came into the group. She became a part of the solution for herself and, in time, for others.

Margaret decided to relocate to the city near the treatment center and halfway house. She had already made so many new friends in that area that it seemed like a natural place to start over. Jeff received a wonderful note from her recently that talked about her gratitude, both for her family, who took action to help her, and the treatment professionals, who got the diagnosis right and thus got her on the road to real recovery.

But the majority of the credit goes to Margaret, who followed the directions of the treatment team and made the difficult choices that ensured her recovery.

These choices included (a) accepting help in the first place, (b) taking the medication in spite of some initial side effects, (c) working hard at the treatment process, (d) accepting the recommendation of a halfway house, and (e) getting involved on a deep level with the local AA group. Because Margaret was willing to take action and apply herself, she succeeded.

6

Bipolar Disorders

Manic depression distorts the moods and thoughts, incites dreadful behaviors, destroys the basis of rational thought, and too often erodes the desire and will to live. It is an illness that is biological in its origin, yet one that feels psychological in the experience of it; an illness that is unique in conferring advantage and pleasure, yet one that brings in its wake almost unendurable suffering and, not infrequently, suicide.

Kay Redfield Jamison, Ph.D.
From *An Unquiet Mind*

Of all the mental health disorders, bipolar disorder is one of the most misdiagnosed. How can we so often miss what can be so devastating? It may have to do with the fact that mania doesn't always manifest itself with wild spending sprees or conversations with God. Or maybe it is the confusing language—it used to be called manic-depressive illness, and now we use labels such as *bipolar I, bipolar II,* and *soft bipolar.* Perhaps people confuse it with the types of depression noted in chapter 5, depression that involves a shift of mood in only one direction (unipolar depression). The mania aspect, or opposite pole, may not be obvious, or may be obscured by inaccurate self-report, selective memory, or the use of mood-altering substances. From a symptomatic viewpoint, the mood changes that characterize bipolar disorder may not seem that severe at first—but how do we define *severe?* The symptoms are also intermittent. Months, years, or even decades can pass between episodes. And to further confuse matters, drug and alcohol addiction can duplicate the symptoms of bipolar disorder. Because of these and other possible reasons, the time span between the first symptom and a correct diagnosis is, on average, eight years—even longer if an addiction is involved.

More than just mood swings, bipolar disorder is defined by instability of mood and a shifting between the two poles of extreme happiness and crushing depression. It is a potentially serious but treatable condition. According to the National Institute of Mental Health (NIMH), about 5.7 million American adults, or about 2.6 percent of the population age eighteen or older, have bipolar disorder in any given year. Starting at any age, and crossing all ethnic and social lines, this condition most definitely runs in family lines. Bipolar disorder is also the mental health condition most associated with suicidal ideation, attempts, and completion. Among people diagnosed with bipolar disorder, suicide completion is estimated at a staggering rate of 10 percent. The odds are even higher when a co-occurring addiction is involved.

Let's take a closer look at the types of bipolar disorder most frequently encountered in dual diagnoses. Following is a brief review of the categories used by diagnosticians.

Bipolar I

This form of bipolar disorder is the most extreme, and, in theory, it should be fairly easy to diagnose. Bipolar I disorder involves full-blown mania, a highly energized, sleep-deprived, exceptionally grandiose, hyperverbal state that often presents with psychotic features. Although depression is part of the picture, the most often-observed determinant for the bipolar I diagnosis is the extent of the mania. The depression may or may not be more severe than other forms of depression or other forms of bipolar disorder. In fact, a person can meet the criteria for bipolar I *without ever having experienced a clinical depression.*

Individuals with bipolar I act and feel as if they are special, God speaks to them, or they are on some direct mission to save the world. They feel incredibly powerful and enlightened, eyes aglow. Someone in full-blown mania, manifesting classic bipolar I, displays some very clear symptoms, including bulging eyes, rapid speech, and grandiose language with distorted reality. People with bipolar I disorder display amazing stamina and can go for days without sleep. They speak rapidly, sometimes making sense, but often they are so energized that they make multiple grandiose statements. They are prone to reckless spending, poor interpersonal judgment, and hypersexual behavior. Some highly charismatic individuals and gifted artists can function productively for periods of time, until their symptoms become too outlandish or they begin to cycle in the other direction. The majority of acute episodes of mania are readily detected, assessed, and treated.

Some mood-altering substances mimic an acute state of mania, and this is where the bipolar diagnosis is sometimes overlooked. Amphetamines, Ecstasy, or cocaine can, for some individuals, produce an acute mania. But the bipolar I disorder, as opposed to a drug-induced mania, precedes or lasts beyond the acute effect of the mood-altering substance.

In some cases, bipolar I symptoms are caused by an endocrine problem, a reaction to a medication, or some other diagnosable medical condition. Bipolar I, or any form of bipolar disorder not attributable to another medical condition, seems to come and go. Some individuals have multiple episodes, others just one. They are sometimes set off by an event or trauma, but often there are no clear or identifiable triggers.

Bipolar I is sometimes misdiagnosed as schizophrenia, which is described more fully in chapter 7. A full-blown manic episode includes psychotic features, but it is different from schizophrenia. Schizophrenia is primarily a disturbance of thought, although it may affect mood. Bipolar I is primarily a disruption of mood that disrupts thought. Although they might look identical, the source of disturbance is different. While most bipolar I psychotic episodes last a relatively short time—a day, a week, and sometimes a month—schizophrenia tends to linger. Regardless, the boundary between these conditions sometimes blurs, and the hybrid diagnosis is called schizoaffective disorder. People with schizoaffective disorder tend to function better than schizophrenics because they go through relatively calm periods. Their baseline thinking tends not to be as severe as the baseline for those with chronic schizophrenia, but their swings in mood definitely affect their ability to function.

In an estimated 20 to 40 percent of bipolar patients, manic episodes are set off by antidepressant medication. In some instances, this is the first indication that a bipolar disorder, not a unipolar depression, is the actual problem. The sudden surge in serotonin can cause a full-blown manic episode that may not have naturally occurred.

Bipolar II

Bipolar II disorder includes both up and down moods, but the mania is not as extreme as with bipolar I. Bipolar II involves a less dramatic form of mania known as hypomania. Hypomanic symptoms include rapid thoughts, a sense of exceptional confidence, decreased sleep, rapid speech (although not necessarily psychotic), jumping around from topic to topic, easy distraction, increased sexuality, and sometimes increased spending. Hypomania need not involve distortions of reality, although in its classic form it often does. Some manifestations of hypomania are hard to distinguish from a strong sense of well-being or from a drug-induced high. Diagnosticians look for indications of hypomania, but too often the symptoms are unreported or underreported. Patients themselves have a hard time distinguishing between hypomania and simply feeling good. Also, a clinical interview may take place during the depression phase of bipolar II, and any report of feeling good may be omitted or reported with such little enthusiasm that the clinician is misinformed.

Depression, the other pole of bipolar II, is easier to identify. Taken alone, the symptoms of a bipolar II depression are really no different from other forms of depression mentioned in the previous chapter. In most instances, bipolar II depressions will not include psychotic features. However, use of drugs or alcohol can result in depression with psychotic features. There are no blood tests to tell us what type of depression we are dealing with. Symptoms of unipolar and bipolar depression can be identical, making the reported presence or absence of mania so important for an accurate diagnosis. How a patient responds to medication can sometimes lead to an accurate diagnosis as well. A very pragmatic psychiatrist once said: "If you give them lithium and they get better, it was bipolar I." A corollary to that is "If you give them an SSRI and they become manic, it was likely bipolar II." It seems that certain individuals who become acutely manic when taking an SSRI may be sensitive to excess serotonin availability, while they do not appear to be as sensitive to antidepressants affecting only norepinephrine. This peculiar phenomenon is not fully understood, nor is it universal.

Getting the right diagnosis, especially when dealing with bipolar illnesses coupled with addiction, requires being open to the fact that the original diagnosis might be wrong. A family's objective observations can be of immeasurable help in discerning which mood disorder, if any, a loved one is dealing with.

Mixed Bipolar

Mixed bipolar occurs when both depression and mania are present at the same time. The individual is energized but extremely sad at the same time. This mixed presentation is sometimes referred to as an agitated depression. The individual is energized, anxious, agitated, and depressed. This is an extremely uncomfortable combination of high energy and definite depression. This mixed state is sometimes associated with medical illness, specifically endocrine or thyroid problems. Occasionally, a specific illness, such as Graves' disease, an autoimmune disorder that causes over-activity of the thyroid gland, can be misconstrued as mixed bipolar. In some instances, what looks like a mixed bipolar disorder is the result of the ingestion of illicit drugs.

Although not a separate category, another form of mixed bipolar includes surges in anxiety coupled with depression, loss of sleep, and agitation. Sometimes considered an atypical, agitated, or complicated depression, this blended state of disquieting agitation can include surges of anger and hypersensitivity.

A less common form of mixed bipolar is the rapid cycling bipolar disorder. More common in women, this variant is associated with swings in mood that can occur several times within a day. Rather than the mixed presentation that involves a blend of depression, negativity, and excessive energy, a person diagnosed with rapid cycling disorder tends to go from depression to mania in short periods of time. She may be vegetative and negative in the morning, then grandiose, energetic, and manic by afternoon. The shift between cycles can be quite sudden, and the rate of change tends to be more rapid with those who are more severely disturbed. Periods of rapid cycling can be brief, or they can plague an individual for months. Women who suffer from rapid cycling become worse, or experience more rapid cycling, during the onset of the menstrual cycle. Similarly, the use of birth control pills can set off rapid cycles or other variants of the bipolar condition.

Cyclothymic Disorder

Cyclothymic disorder, or cyclothymia, is a less dramatic form of bipolar disorder. Moods swing between hypomania and depression but are not too severe or long-lasting. The rate of cycling is variable and often slower. The intensity of the ups and downs does not meet the criteria for bipolar I or II, yet the disorder can be described as more than normal moodiness. These swings in mood, as with all bipolar disorders, are not clearly linked to external events. However, certain events and changes in health or diet can affect the intensity and duration of the cycles. Individuals who suffer from cyclothymia are often able to function without significant social consequences. They do not necessarily wind up in hospitals. Due to confusion in diagnosis, as well as denial on the patient's part, cyclothymia can be overlooked or underreported. In some instances, a history of cyclothymia is observed before a possible progression to bipolar I or bipolar II disorder. However, cyclothymic disorder does not necessarily predict or precede bipolar disorder.

It is very easy to misattribute the mood anomalies of cyclothymia to illicit chemicals or alcohol. A family history of mood disorder or a history of cyclothymia before onset of addiction can make this diagnosis slightly easier.

Atypical Bipolar Disorder

People who have features of bipolar disorder but fail to meet exact diagnostic criteria for bipolar I, bipolar II, mixed bipolar, or cyclothymia are put into the category of atypical bipolar. Some creative professionals have advocated the use of the terms *bipolar 2.5* or *bipolar III*. The atypical bipolar diagnosis fits those who "fall between the cracks," or those who have not yet developed the full-blown types of bipolar illness.

A person with atypical bipolar is generally moody, is sometimes impulsive, and may have some of the characteristics we often associate with addiction. Their mania, for example, may only be reflected in a single symptom: failure to sleep. The failure to sleep alone does not warrant an atypical bipolar diagnosis, but it could be a soft indicator of mania that would not otherwise reach diagnostic criteria. In other instances, a failure to concentrate and focus, which looks identical to attention deficit disorder, may be connected to an atypical bipolar. Patients often are suddenly able to focus when given a mood stabilizer instead of or together with an antidepressant or stimulant. Many individuals who suffer from PTSD or its complex variant CPTSD (discussed in chapter 9) have low-grade atypical bipolar disorder. The inability to moderate emotion, or "affect"—sometimes called "affective storms"—may not ease until a mood stabilizer is prescribed. Atypical bipolar disorder may also be a factor in an eating disorder that has not responded to other treatment approaches. Some clinicians believe that atypical bipolar disorder plays a role in chronic relapsing of addictive disorders. Since mood regulation is an underpinning of so many conditions, the possibility that an atypical bipolar disorder is present can be an important consideration.

It is not clear how many individuals suffer from atypical bipolar disorder, but it may be that this is the most common and most difficult bipolar disorder to diagnose. Many of the so-called constitutionally incapable addicts—those with a history of multiple relapses—can fall into this pool of atypical mood disorders. It is our suspicion that the atypical variant of the bipolar disorder is where nature (genetic loading) and environment (damage due to drugs and events) meet at the halfway point. It may eventually be discerned that large numbers of addicts in general suffer from atypical mood disorders. The distinct boundaries that we use for diagnosis may be called into question as our understanding of the enormous complexity of mood regulation and atypical mood disorders improves.

Biological Aspects

Although environment (e.g., stressful events, head injury, and drug-related brain injury) can play a role in bipolar disorders, it is widely accepted that bipolar disorder is a brain disease and is mostly the consequence of genetic factors. Most studies estimate that 70 to 80 percent of people diagnosed with a bipolar disorder (not including the atypical bipolar condition) carry the disorder in their genes, a percentage well above the usual 60 percent seen in other disorders, including addiction.

The familial linkage of these disorders was first documented in the 1940s, and the bipolar condition is considered the foundation for modern biogenetic behavioral research. Although the specific genetics is still being investigated, the majority of practitioners accept that bipolar conditions have a powerful genetic and biological underpinning. As of this writing, there is still no reliable blood test, medical test, or specific genetic marker that can identify who is at risk for this powerfully disruptive condition. Eventually, specific types of imaging may permit physicians to see bipolar disorders, at least while they are active.

One theory about bipolar disorders is that they are related to an electrochemical scramble similar to what happens in the brain during a seizure. Known as the kindling theory, this model suggests that the brain undergoes flares when mania or irritability is present and that the severity of bipolar disorder increases over time and includes effects from hormones. Although not proven, the kindling theory links to one clear fact: Many individuals who suffer from bipolar disorders respond favorably to anticonvulsant medications. Antiseizure medicines also seem to help manage impulse disorders and anger disorders. The models, mechanisms, and theories around bipolar disorders are still being developed. Although mysteries remain, the genetics, proteins, and mechanics of this disease will likely be decoded in our lifetimes.

Psychological Aspects

Bipolar illness can have a profound psychological impact. Episodes may disrupt thinking, beliefs, goals, and work efficiency. Self-esteem, decision making, and follow-through are all affected by this powerful disorder. Those dealing with bipolar disorders struggle for control—control of their minds, of themselves, and, in some instances, of their reality. Many have described the challenge as trying to build a dwelling on shifting sand. Perceptions may be more intense, opinions more extreme, and the context of perception and memory dramatically impacted.

Some people become driven. They invest their intensity, curiosity, and sensitivity into career or artistic pursuits. During the hypomanic phase, they may be capable of outstanding achievement. Many famous individuals have suffered with this disorder. Kay Redfield Jamison's *Touched with Fire* highlights the lives of artists, poets, scholars, and musicians who have had this disorder. A brief list of contemporary sufferers includes Patty Duke, Margot Kidder, James Taylor, Buzz Aldrin, Francis Ford Coppola, and Tim Burton. It is widely believed that Winston Churchill was bipolar, not just a victim of "the black dog" mentioned in the last chapter. Some speculate that Abraham Lincoln also had a bipolar disorder.

For those who suffer from discernable mania or hypomania, the loss of intensity can be crushing. For those who cycle into depressive episodes, it may feel as if the world is about to end and that life has no meaning. The shifts back and forth can be very confusing. Relationships suffer, and mixed signals become part of the interpersonal language.

Spiritual Aspects

It is believed by many that some inspired historical figures, military leaders, visionaries, cult leaders, and religious founders were radiantly aglow as a consequence of manic episodes. It is widely believed that many of the false messiahs throughout history suffered from mania; others may have had schizoaffective disorders. More ordinary folks dealing with the bipolar condition may feel as if they have been selected by God one day but then abandoned and empty a few months later. The relationship with one's Higher Power may be disrupted and confused. During a manic phase, boundaries and beliefs may be exaggerated, followed by a crashing shift into emptiness, hopelessness, and meaninglessness.

Those who suffer from the more common bipolar II may have less extreme experiences, but they, too, may have a similar loss of faith or inability to stay focused on the concept of a supreme being. While some individuals may feel closer to a Higher Power by having experienced a higher feeling of connectedness, others become skeptical and cynical. The question of powerlessness and acceptance of either the bipolar condition and/or an addictive disorder is complicated by the more extreme experiences associated with mood disorders. The soothing impact of a spiritual system likely contributes to mood stability and a sense of well-being.

Treating Bipolar Disorders

Biological Methods

Three types of medication are used to treat bipolar illness. The first medication, lithium, belongs in a class by itself. Lithium is an element and is usually prescribed in a salt form, lithium carbonate, or more commonly as a timed-release version called Lithobid.

Mineral waters were long believed to be helpful in soothing the agitated, infirmed, or confused. It was believed that the minerals put the "aqueous humors" back into balance. The ancient Greeks believed that diseases were treated by restoring balance to bodily fluids such as water, bile, and blood. During the 1940s, Australian psychiatrist John Cade began a search for a biological treatment for mental illness and discovered the dramatic effects of lithium carbonate. Due to the toxicity of lithium, the use of lithium for bipolar illness was delayed until the late 1950s. Lithium today is still considered the gold standard for treating bipolar disorders.

Lithium dosage must be carefully monitored; it is not quickly broken down in the body and does not immediately take effect. Lithium works extremely well, but it does have several side effects. Many individuals who take it gain weight, and if it is used in high doses over many years, it can adversely affect the kidneys. It also causes a slight tremor for some. Lithium in very high doses is also extremely toxic and can be fatal if used in a suicide attempt. Nobody knows exactly why lithium is effective.

The second group of medications is the anticonvulsants, medications originally created to treat epilepsy but also used to treat other brain injuries, including Parkinson's disease. Anticonvulsants include Depakote, Dilantin, Tegretol, Neurontin, Trileptal, and Lamictal. Topamax, another widely used anticonvulsant, and Gabritril are also sometimes utilized, although some studies suggest Topamax is not highly effective as a mood stabilizer. Topamax may, however, be extremely helpful in preventing relapse urges for addicts.

Although all of these medications act as anticonvulsants, they all have slightly different properties and effects. Depakote has more of a sedating effect and is highly useful for those who suffer from mania and hypomania. Lamictal appears to be helpful to those who are prone to bipolar depression. Anticonvulsants appear to work very well and have relatively few and generally mild side effects. Finding which medication will be most effective for an individual can be a matter of trial and error. Why anticonvulsants help with bipolar disorders is still not clear; the discovery was accidental.

The third and most recently added group of medications approved for use with bipolar disorders is the atypical antipsychotics (sometimes called neuroleptics), which were developed in the 1990s. Effective for schizoaffective disorders, these medications have a definite calming effect, not a desirable consequence if depression is the major symptom. Critics observe that atypical antipsychotic medications are overprescribed to populations who have disorders other than schizophrenia. Antipsychotics can help specific types of disorders and specific episodes within the bipolar illness, but they may not be appropriate across the board. Antipsychotic medications can have significant medical side effects. These medications should only be prescribed after careful thought and consideration. The smallest dose possible for the shortest duration is usually the best approach, but the final choice should be made after careful discussion with the prescribing physician. In more severe presentations of bipolar illness, atypical antipsychotics can be invaluable. However, as has been the case for other medications, the newer medications may not be as effective or risk free as originally promoted.

Although the medications available have side effects and there is still some uncertainty as to how they work, we are fortunate to live in an era where we can intervene effectively with powerful medication and combinations of medications that can contribute to a much-improved quality of life for those who have bipolar disorder. Recent studies suggest that lithium and anticonvulsants are associated with complete remission in symptoms for 30 to 40 percent of those who use them. The remaining percentages receive significant relief, but doses and medicines need to be managed more closely. As we strive to improve outcomes, evidence-based biological treatments face many challenges. It is hoped that we will soon understand what causes these conditions so that newer, more targeted therapies can provide even better results with fewer side effects. Research is under way that looks at regions of the brain affected by specific subtypes of the disorder and how medicines affect those areas.

Even more exciting are the discoveries yet to be made in terms of the addiction process as it is connected to mood balance and the biochemical circuits involved. Medication that works for stabilizing mood may in the future help us to better treat addiction to mood-altering substances.

Psychological Methods

Lives, careers, relationships, and confidence are frequent casualties of bipolar disorder. The clarity, objectivity, and guidance of a mental health professional providing psychotherapy can help maintain rational thinking, goals, clarity, and balance, as well as provide reassuring feedback. Many individuals who suffer from bipolar disorder operate from a position of fear and denial. A good clinician will teach patients skills of self-management, sometimes referred to as "teaching them to become better self-scientists." Mastering skills is healing. In addition, a healthy source of trusted support may interrupt suicidal impulses.

Psychotherapy can help prevent relapse for addiction and bipolar disorder. Often, the psychotherapist is the first person to observe when a mania or a depression is beginning and can encourage rapid action, such as changes in medication or dosage.

Lifestyle and Nutritional Factors

Environment and lifestyle factors may delay the onset of bipolar illness, just as diet may delay the onset of type 2 diabetes or heart disease. Even for those who suffer with full-blown bipolar disorder and take medication, lifestyle and environmental factors can be very powerful in helping to manage the condition and to prevent episodes. The following suggestions are worthy of consideration:

1. Maintain daily structure and routine. Boredom and overwork should be avoided. Those who are prone to mood disorders appear to require consistency, routine, and structure. A regular sleep schedule may help manage hormonal and biochemical ups and downs. People who have or are at risk for bipolar disorders should probably not work flexible shifts, and some may not wish to work night shifts. Whatever appears to fit, whether a day or night shift, should remain consistent, if at all possible.

2. Be careful of emotional jolts. Seek support, help, and medication management if affected by an emotional shock or jolt, such as the loss of a relationship or the death of a loved one.

3. Get daily exercise and fresh air. A simple, healthy regimen is logical and necessary for those dealing with, or at risk for, bipolar disorder. Sunshine provides vital vitamin D for the body. (Many foods contain vitamin D, but there is evidence that some sunshine, best ob-

tained on a twenty- to thirty-minute daily walk in the morning or late afternoon, also boosts mood.) A short daily walk also helps to regulate mood and prevent depression. People with a history of bipolar I or a family history of mania may wish to avoid rigorous exercise, which may set off mania.

4. Watch your diet. Some bipolar episodes or bipolar relapses can be connected to too many servings of highly caffeinated coffee. Be aware that light roasts have more caffeine than dark roasts and that certain brands and brews contain much more caffeine than others. Also, know that some clear beverages are loaded with caffeine. Individuals at risk for bipolar illness should avoid or abstain from caffeine. Similarly, diets that contain too much sugar or quickly metabolized carbohydrates may set off mood-changing episodes. A healthy, balanced diet high in protein is probably most judicious. We highly recommend working closely with a qualified nutritionist.

   Omega-3 essential fatty acids are worthy of particular emphasis. Evidence demonstrates that these oils, found in fish, walnuts, canola oil, olive oil, soybean products, and flax seeds, appear to be potent regulators of mood. These essential acids also help to keep the heart healthy. There is even evidence to suggest that omega-3 consumption lowers suicide risk. Again, we recommend consulting with a nutritionist and obtaining a sufficient dosage of omega-3 fats. Final words of caution: Be sure your sources for omega-3 are sufficiently pure and potent. Many nutritionists recommend pharmaceutical-grade fish oils, for example. Also, do not substitute nutritional additives for medicine, and, obviously, inform the psychiatrist or physician you work with if you are taking any natural supplements, including omega-3s. Any herbal, nutritional, or natural intervention must be reported to your doctor.

Support Groups

Dual Disorders Anonymous and Dual Recovery Anonymous are Twelve Step groups in which peers discuss the challenges of accepting both addiction and psychiatric diagnoses. In addition, the Depression and Bipolar Support Alliance (formerly known as the National Depressive/Manic Depressive Association), the National Alliance for the Mentally Ill, the National Mental Health Association, and Recovery, Inc., all hold meetings for people suffering from bipolar disorder. The Twelve Step meetings deal with both conditions, but, in some instances, going to condition-specific meetings may better fit individual needs. The dynamics and resources vary with each community. People are often reluctant to join groups, but these meetings save people's lives every day. Individuals realize that they are not unique, that they must accept the reality of their condition(s), and that support systems are there to help them get through denial, passivity, and isolation.

Blurring the Lines

As we noted in the beginning of this chapter, it often takes years and sometimes decades for a bipolar diagnosis to be made. Even experts miss this diagnosis, and they miss it every day. Recurrent relapsing due to drug or alcohol use may be connected to an untreated or undertreated bipolar condition, often the atypical kind. Conversely, some bipolar conditions may be the consequence of brain damage associated with long-term drug use. Individuals with bipolar disorders are more likely to have problems with concentration; there may be a link between ADD/ADHD and the eventual development of bipolar disorders. Mood anomalies may not fit precisely within the guidelines and diagnostic criteria. Mania may be displayed by anger outbursts, agitation, or lack of sleep. Grandiosity, a telltale symptom of mania, may not be present in some episodes. Depressions that are part of the bipolar disorder may be indistinguishable from unipolar depression. Anxiety symptoms may also be part of the clinical presentation.

Although the science is not yet clear, it appears that some bipolar disorders are set off as a result of substance use, abuse, or addiction. There are reported incidents of mood disorders starting as a consequence of the use of prednisone for skin disorders; Jane Pauley's memoir *Skywriting: A Life Out of the Blue* describes this very process. Would she have developed a bipolar condition had the steroid not been prescribed? Who knows? The reality is that it is possible that substance use, abuse, or addiction will set into motion a mood disorder that might or might not have otherwise appeared. We believe that certain chemicals, particularly MDMA (Ecstasy), methamphetamines, cocaine, and perhaps even alcohol, may set off an underlying mood disorder; it depends on individual genetic vulnerability to the chemical, as well as the degree of vulnerability to the mood disorder.

Can a mood disorder set off an addictive disorder? We do not know for sure, nor is there any definitive study that shows causation. The only thing we have to work with right now is correlation. However, based on clinical experience, it seems possible that people with a lower genetic loading for addiction might be more vulnerable to addiction because they seek out street substances to self-medicate depression or mania. Those substances may then accelerate the mood disorder and, in turn, may result in even more use of addictive chemicals. It is possible that the lines between addiction and mood dysfunction are more blurred and interconnected than we ever imagined. The definitive answers may take decades, but our clinical thinking must include multiple possibilities.

Recommendations

Bipolar disorders and addiction appear to be connected, but no one is exactly sure how. Their symptoms overlap, their course overlaps, and one exacerbates the other. As with all co-occurring conditions, lifelong abstinence is the first requirement. Anyone who is at risk for bipolar disorder should abstain from mood-altering chemicals.

Because bipolar disorders vary in their presentation, frequency, and intensity, keep the flow of information clear to providers. Rely on the clinical and diagnostic practitioner's judgment, but do not be afraid to add information and pose challenging questions. You should also take time to learn all you can about bipolar disorders. There is a wealth of information available, despite the fact that you may lack core understanding. If you get the sense that you are getting "cookie-cutter" treatment or "rubber-stamp" diagnoses, you need to seek out other opinions. Use all of the support available, learn more about the disorder, and attend specific bipolar support groups. Higher levels of care, inpatient treatment, psychiatric stabilization, and residential extended care may be necessary. Finally, work closely with addiction professionals and the prescribing physicians, and maximize the environmental and nutritional suggestions we have provided. Co-occurring addiction and mood disorders require scrupulous work, flexibility in thinking, and assertive utilization of multidisciplinary service providers. Although neither condition can be cured, both can be successfully managed.

We hope better informed family members can help caregivers accelerate a correct diagnosis and support the proper levels of comprehensive, multidisciplinary care. Be informed, be assertive, and maintain your clarity, your emotional balance, and, above all, your positive attitude.

Case History

Rick was a star. He had earned a law degree, passed the bar, and gotten a high-paying corporate position before the age of thirty. There seemed to be no limit to what he might accomplish, until he started having volatile moods. Friends and family hardly knew what to think. It seemed as though he had reached a mountaintop and then fallen off.

By the time he was thirty-seven, his behavior was erratic. After having been a model of responsibility, he became incapable of keeping a schedule, meeting deadlines, or following through on projects. He lost interest in his social life and became obsessed with arcane subjects such as the Mayan legal system.

Rick always had a powerful and assertive personality, but he became aggressive and threatening, running off one girlfriend after another. Complaints came from his subordinates, too, and there were threats of harassment charges. His superiors also found him difficult to work with, not only because of his deteriorating performance but also because of his loud and irrational defense of his behavior.

Finally, he quit his job, took up residence in a small apartment, and delved deeper into his Mayan research, which he proclaimed to be revolutionary. By this time, he was drinking at least twelve beers every day, and sometimes much more. He vacillated between great enthusiasm for his research— including many all-night sessions of reading and writing—and a complete inability to get out of bed or take care of simple chores such as cooking and laundry. He was also running out of money.

Rick's family tried to reason with him, but to no avail. He refused to look for work or address his financial problems. Although he was gentle around children and family pets, he became argumentative on any subject that pertained to him. He was physically intimidating, although never violent. His friends and family became increasingly worried that he was losing touch with reality.

Finally, the family decided to intervene. It was obvious that Rick wouldn't address his problems on his own, so they had to take action. His family didn't know exactly what was wrong with him, but they wanted a team of professionals to come up with a clear diagnosis and a long-term treatment plan.

The interventionist (Jeff Jay) spent a good deal of time getting a complete history from family members and friends. The information suggested that Rick was probably bipolar and also drank alcoholically. Still, there were many unanswered questions about the origin of his problems.

Rick did not start drinking a lot until his bipolar disorder came along. Although there was some family history of alcoholism, Rick's family had never seen him intoxicated until the mental health problem surfaced. In this case, the bipolar disorder did not cause alcoholism, but rather it provided a triggering event that caused Rick to drink more. Once he began drinking at a high daily level, his alcoholism emerged.

Because Rick had become paranoid and reclusive, the interventionist decided against the typical group intervention technique. Instead, an executive-style intervention was prepared, which would consist largely of one-to-one sessions with Rick and the interventionist.

The interventionist met with Rick for an extended period of time, without getting an agreement for treatment. The meeting was continued the next day, again for a long period of time and again without a successful conclusion. At this point, a structured intervention, including many family members, was scheduled for the following day. The next morning—day three of the intervention process—the family intervention took place. The process was much easier than the family expected, and it provided just the added impetus necessary for Rick to agree to treatment. He and Jeff left for the treatment center the same day.

Rick stayed in treatment for one month and then moved on to an extended care facility that specialized in co-occurring disorders. One of the most noticeable changes came right away when he began a regular exercise program. When combined with a healthy diet and supplements, his mood became naturally elevated, and he regained much of his old fire. His bipolar disorder was successfully treated with medication and psychotherapy, and his alcoholism was addressed through the Twelve Steps of Alcoholics Anonymous. Rick started making friends in AA, and he attended one meeting every day.

More than two years after his treatment began, Rick is abstinent from alcohol, deeply involved in AA, and continuing to take a prescribed medication. He holds an executive position again and is enjoying life. Although he was initially resistant to the intervention, he is now a strong advocate for treatment.

"I was ready to kill that interventionist when he first suggested treatment," says Rick. "But deep down, I knew he was right. I was falling apart, but I didn't know what to do about it. And why should I know what to do about it? I was the sick person. I couldn't be the doctor too!"

7

Psychosis

One morning, as Gregor Samsa was waking up from anxious dreams, he discovered that in bed he had been changed into a monstrous verminous bug. He lay on his armour-hard back and saw, as he lifted his head up a little, his brown, arched abdomen divided up into rigid bow-like sections. From this height the blanket, just about ready to slide off completely, could hardly stay in place. His numerous legs, pitifully thin in comparison to the rest of his circumference, flickered helplessly before his eyes.
"What's happened to me," he thought. It was no dream.

Franz Kafka
From *The Metamorphosis*

In classic literature, sorting out what is real from what is not real is the heart of a good story. For millions of families, it is a living nightmare. From the vantage point of the family members, the challenge is deciphering whether they are dealing with a real mental illness, the effects of drugs or alcohol, or both. Professionals have a hard time making this distinction as well. Unless we are looking at a fully developed addiction or mental illness, differentiating one from the other can be difficult.

Psychosis, also referred to as a disturbance in thinking, is a broad, descriptive term that involves impairment in perception, behavior, and emotion. It includes hallucinations and/or delusions that can be visual, auditory, tactile, and olfactory. Psychotic reactions can be temporary or long lasting, and many things besides addiction and mental illness can cause psychosis.

Many healthy people have had temporary psychotic episodes. After two or three days without sleep, people are likely to experience distortions of perception, including hallucinations. It has long been believed that normal sleep is what keeps us from becoming psychotic. People can also have a psychotic experience when they have a fever or a bad reaction to a medicine or food toxins. Psychosis can also be the consequence of extreme intoxication. Numerous medical conditions, including certain head injuries, Parkinson's disease, AIDS, malaria, dementia, and syphilis, can result in a lasting psychosis.

The level of anxiety experienced during a psychotic episode is unforgettable and transcends ordinary anxiety. Harry Stack Sullivan, a pioneering early twentieth-century psychiatrist, described the experience as "uncanny anxiety." According to Sullivan, the intense level of anxiety occurs when someone has a breakdown of ego integrity, meaning the ego no longer functions as the core of thought, reality, identity, or sense of self. Quite simply, it is the process of losing one's mind. Many times, there is a loss of who we are, where we are, and a sense of time.

Addiction and Psychosis

Mood-altering chemicals induce changes in thinking. When individuals talk about getting high, they often use the phrase "getting out of my head." Uncle Leo does not dance with the lamp shade using clear thinking. When he is "under the influence," mood as well as thoughts are disjointed and disturbed. Many alcoholics have impeccable logic while drunk; the ability to handle large quantities of alcohol, at least at first, is actually one of the hallmarks of alcoholism. The eventual course of alcoholism, however, involves profound brain cell damage, which can lead to a specific type of psychosis known as *wet brain*. The degree of deterioration involves a complex collision of substance choice, frequency of use, and genetic vulnerability to brain damage and psychotic disorders. The combinations and possibilities are endless. The most extreme cases are easier to identify. The symptoms are classic: hallucinations, delusions, illogical conversations, hearing voices, talking to oneself, memory loss, poor self-care, lack of social functioning, and poor interpersonal boundaries. This neurological decline is often reversible with sobriety, but if untreated, it will eventually result in dementia and/or Korsakoff's psychosis, a particularly virulent form of psychosis.

Many of the psychotic symptoms experienced during the late stages of alcoholism are similar to those experienced by someone who is high on hallucinogens, including LSD, mushrooms, locoweed, and marijuana, or stimulants such as cocaine, amphetamines, and methamphetamines.

Drugs have been around for a long time, but these days youngsters are being exposed to harsher chemical mixtures at earlier ages. Some neurologists believe that young brains may be more vulnerable to permanent damage. More potent drugs are being ingested, often heavily, during adolescence or even preadolescence.

Most addicts use alcohol and one or more other drugs. Pot is more potent than it was in the 1960s, cocaine is widely used, and club drugs such as Ecstasy (MDMA), ketamine, GHB, and Rohypnol are incredibly powerful and get mixed in frightening combinations, along with alcohol. Neurological evidence shows that Ecstasy and methamphetamine damage serotonin receptors. Today's addicts are also snorting painkillers, huffing chemicals, and using combinations that were not conceived of a generation ago. Pot is also laced with hallucinogens and sometimes with mysterious substances that cause psychotic-like effects and possible brain injury. The potency of today's drugs may be, in part, why we are seeing a noticeable increase in the complexity of symptoms, diagnoses, and resistance to recovery.

While addicts might seek altered states of reality, if the "trip" is bad or does not end, the anxiety experienced is dreadful. A recovering colleague, who is a Vietnam veteran with many traumatic encounters, said: "The most traumatic thing I have ever experienced was a bad acid trip; the best way I can describe it is my ego disintegrated."

Many addicts who experience psychotic episodes, bad trips, and loss of ego integrity are disoriented enough to be assaulted without being aware of it. MDMA, a powerful hallucinogen, is often involved in episodes of sexual assault. This adds additional layers of confusion and complexity in terms of trust, judgment, boundaries, and accurate thinking.

Psychotic Disorders

The term *psychotic disorder* is a general diagnostic category that incorporates specific conditions. Schizophrenia is one type of psychosis. The different psychotic disorders involve varying levels of disturbed thought and perception. We focus on schizophrenia because, with this mental illness, psychosis is the most prevalent and defining symptom.

Schizophrenia

Schizophrenia is a chronic brain disease that appears in about 1 percent of the worldwide population. Its causes are not known, and it can be a debilitating condition, although some modern therapies improve symptoms in ways that were unimaginable a few decades ago. Individuals with schizophrenia sometimes use mood-altering substances to manage their disease, and this makes symptoms worse. There are several different types of schizophrenia.

Paranoid schizophrenia is a dramatic form of psychosis that includes persecutory thinking and fully developed delusions. The paranoid schizophrenic usually hears voices and believes he is the center of some elaborate conspiracy or is being pursued by others in a fashion that is not consistent with reality.

Disorganized schizophrenia, which used to be called hebephrenic schizophrenia, is characterized by disorganized speech and behavior and flat affect. There is an absence of a consistent theme—a hallmark difference from the well-organized delusions seen with paranoid schizophrenia. The paranoid schizophrenic tends to have a fully developed delusional system with a coherent theme (believing, for example, that aliens are landing), while the disorganized schizophrenic's delusions are not as cohesive or as consistent.

Catatonic schizophrenia is characterized by bizarre alterations in speech, movement, and posturing. Catatonic schizophrenics sometimes remain frozen and speechless for long periods of time.

Undifferentiated schizophrenia includes a mixed presentation of delusions, changes in speech and movement, and disorganized behavior that does not fit the other categories.

Less common categories, including residual schizophrenia, schizophreniform disorder, and brief psychotic disorder, are also considered when making a specific diagnosis.

Common to most forms of schizophrenia are delusions and hallucinations—visual, auditory, tactile, and olfactory—which are called positive symptoms, or symptoms that we look for. Negative symptoms include flatness of emotion, deficiencies in self-care, and inability to experience pleasure. The specific types of hallucinations give diagnosticians and neurologists some good clues as to what type of schizophrenia is involved or whether the psychosis is due to another cause, such as a head injury, medication toxicity, illness, or disease.

Schizophrenia also involves changes in emotional and interpersonal behavior. Normal boundaries aren't observed. Schizophrenics often show a blunted affect; they seem to lose enthusiasm and speak without much emotion, except during periods of agitation or paranoid thinking. They tend to lack insight, display a drop in hygiene, and have difficulty with coherent, sequential thoughts. They tend to make up words, engage in peculiar puns, and make references that leave others befuddled. In its full-blown form, schizophrenia is profoundly disruptive and disabling.

Schizophrenics are no more likely to be violent than the rest of the population, but they are more likely to be addicted, poor, and in prison. The rate of inappropriate and sometimes illegal behavior goes up when diagnosed schizophrenics stop taking their medication or start taking addictive substances.

Schizophrenia most often begins in late adolescence or early adulthood. Many experts on adolescents will note that psychological testing for normal children looks rather schizophrenic at around age thirteen. Although some of the nuances may be the same, there is an unmistakable difference between normal development and the onset of schizophrenia. When drugs are involved, however, the picture becomes much less clear. Schizophrenia is believed to be a genetic illness, but its origins and specific genetic location are not yet clear. Despite decades of research, the cause(s) of schizophrenia are still unknown. People used to believe that bad mothering, specifically from an abusive or violent mother, caused a failure to bond and resulted in schizophrenia. Later theories blamed unhealthy family dynamics—lots of fighting, poor interpersonal boundaries, and "damned if you do, damned if you don't" parental and family rules. This is no longer considered the cause. It was also believed that emotional shock could cause schizophrenia. While shock can result in temporary psychosis, as well as a host of other emotional consequences, the classic "descent into madness" following a shock is considered to be myth by most modern observers.

It is clear that schizophrenia has a genetic and biochemical cause that appears to involve several genes and more than one neurotransmitter. Scientists are now using brain imaging to better understand schizophrenia and whether specific areas of the brain are injured or impaired. Some recent evidence suggests shrinkage in a specific part of the limbic system known as the hippocampus. The imaging results are very preliminary and do not yet give us a definite answer.

The most logical theory about the cause of schizophrenia is called the diathesis-stress model. *Diathesis-stress* refers to the blend of genetics and environment. As with other disorders, it appears that vulnerability is passed on through the genes and that the genes are set into motion by a collision with the environment. The environmental collision may be viral. One of the old theories about schizophrenia is that mothers who experience a flu during pregnancy would have offspring more likely to develop schizophrenia. While there is some statistical evidence supporting this observation, a causal connection has not been established. Other stressors are believed to play a role in setting off schizophrenia, including disappointments during adolescence, family violence, or going to war. Correlations abound, and logic suggests that events may set symptoms in motion, but direct causal mechanisms remain elusive. Perhaps the newest environmental factor worthy of serious consideration is the early use of more consequential mood-altering substances. Young people are exposing immature brains to toxic substances that are known to damage the brain. In other words, the drugs our kids are taking may result in an increased risk for schizophrenia. Some preliminary evidence supports this idea.

Some researchers are suggesting that schizophrenia be dropped from the next volume of the *Diagnostic and Statistical Manual of Mental Disorders (DSM)* and be replaced with dopamine dysregulation disorder. This label may simplify our conceptualization of this confusing and stigmatizing brain disease. It also permits us to better account for the multiple pathways that connect environment, toxins, genetics, and injury to the onset of these disorders.

Drugs, Alcohol, and Brain Injury

Drugs are broken down into three main categories: hallucinogens, stimulants, and depressants. Although hallucinogens are most often associated with hallucinations during use, all mood-altering drugs have the capability of producing psychotic reactions in some people.

Hallucinogens

The 1936 movie *Reefer Madness* depicted people "going mad" when smoking weed and listening to jazz. The movie exaggerated marijuana to such an extent that the film was laughed at in the 1960s and is still considered a cult classic. Ironically, new research is suggesting that chronic use of marijuana, a hallucinogen, may result in increased risk for a variety of psychoses. There is no clear causal mechanism, but the results have been consistent in more than thirty studies. At least one researcher in the Netherlands estimates that as many as 13 percent of all schizophrenia cases are caused by adolescent brains being exposed to powerful cannabinoids, the main chemical in marijuana. The concentration of cannabinoids in marijuana in the early twenty-first century is many times higher than it was forty years ago. In addition, the age of first use has dropped dramatically. A large percentage of the clients we see tell us they smoked their first joint in grade school, some as young as nine years old. Some young people have their first joint with an adult—a neighbor or their parents. As we better understand the cause of psychosis, we will most likely learn how marijuana, as well as other chemicals, can increase the likelihood of schizophrenia.

LSD was at one time thought to be a therapeutic agent for schizophrenia and alcoholism. Even though the results never supported this notion, there remain a few pockets of determined promoters and professionals who insist that hallucinogens can be therapeutic agents. Ibogaine, a hallucinogenic South African weed, has been promoted as a treatment for relapsing addicts, as well as for trauma-related conditions. MDMA (Ecstasy) is currently being used as an experimental therapy for the treatment of post-traumatic stress disorder, including on some veterans. This is clearly an instance of adding insult to injury. Hallucinogens are powerful mood-altering and mind-altering agents. We do not know exactly how they work, but we do know they are addictive. There appear to be some individuals who consume hallucinogens and do not have long-lasting effects. Others take one hit (as in Ashley's case in chapter 1) and begin a path to serious mental illness. Although it is considered rare, a growing number of drug users are experiencing hallucinogen persisting perception disorder (HPPD), the condition we discussed in the first chapter. HPPD can mimic psychosis, cause tremendous anxiety, and trigger relapses. Most clinicians fail to ask about it, and many patients are afraid to volunteer information about their symptoms.

Stimulants

Amphetamines, methamphetamine, and cocaine are stimulants that can induce hallucinations. Amphetamines have been used as medicines for many years. They stimulate dopamine production, which has some clinical utility in treating narcolepsy, attention deficit disorder, and obesity. They are potentially addictive and can easily be misused. The speed with which they enter the bloodstream determines whether they have a therapeutic effect or create a high. Addicts will sometime crush and snort medicinal amphetamines, a dangerous practice. Methamphetamine is an illegal substance processed for maximum rate of absorption. It creates a devastating and quick high, causing damage to many organ systems.

The misuse of amphetamines and the addictive use of methamphetamine cause brain damage. There is even a specific diagnosis for this misuse: amphetamine-induced psychosis. Among the most mentally disturbed people we have seen are those who have been damaged by methamphetamine, a drug that damages serotonin and dopamine cells in the brain. These individuals sometimes become frozen in repetitive, meaningless behaviors. The chemicals ravage the skin, brain, and other organ systems. For many, bodies and minds may never fully recover. Given the increasing rate of the methamphetamine epidemic and the yet-unknown incidence of permanent damage, we do not yet have statistics. Our suspicion is that more than a few psychotic individuals, especially those diagnosed with paranoid schizophrenia, are products of methamphetamine and amphetamine injury.

Sustained use of the stimulant cocaine, especially crack cocaine, can cause what is referred to as a cocaine-induced psychosis. Those who are high on crack or cocaine may experience hallucinations and delusions; this is more common with crack cocaine because it enters the system more rapidly, producing an intense high and damaging serotonin cells. It is not uncommon for users to hear walls speaking, voices behind the bushes, or the police following them. A well-known phenomenon of "crumbing" involves addicts obsessively combing through the carpet seeking the most minute remnant of the drug, real or imagined.

Depressants

Alcohol, a depressant, has mood- and thought-modifying properties, and those who suffer from schizophrenia are much more likely to develop an alcohol dependency. It is not definitively known why alcohol tends to be favored by those suffering from chronic schizophrenia, but some researchers believe alcohol's effect on the dopamine system results in temporary relief from psychotic symptoms. Those who are schizophrenic and alcoholic are at much higher risk for institutionalization, homelessness, or jail.

Can alcohol use or dependence cause schizophrenia? The answers are not very clear. Alcohol consumption during pregnancy, especially when the result is fetal alcohol syndrome, is considered by some to be a possible factor in the development of schizophrenia, but this connection appears to be weak. It is possible that alcohol is a very specific environmental toxin that sets off a genetically vulnerable person to develop schizophrenia, but there haven't been any controlled studies to support this.

Treating the Co-occurring Disorder: Psychosis and Addiction

Psychotic symptoms cause great concern for patients, families, and clinicians. Treating psychosis requires a thorough diagnosis and a solid treatment plan. Understanding the origins of the disorder is important in managing acute symptoms and preventing additional deterioration. The following steps need to be considered in the treatment process:

Abstinence

Getting clean and sober is the very first step in recovery and treatment for addiction and for mental illness. Proper evaluation and treatment can only start after the afflicted person stops using mood-altering chemicals. Once a thinking disturbance is in remission, life does not magically stay better. Abstinence is a vital part of a biological treatment for thinking disturbances that co-occur with substance dependence, regardless of the source of the disturbance.

Medication

It has been said that medication permitted the unlocking of the doors of the old-style mental institutions. Medication provides a much-improved range of management of schizophrenia. The older antipsychotics included Thorazine, Haldol, loxapine, Stelazine, and Prolixin. In recent years, a whole new list of medications has appeared. Clozaril, considered by many to be a revolutionary medicine because of its ability to reduce psychotic symptoms, can only be used as a last resort because of some life-threatening side effects and cumbersome monitoring. Newer antipsychotics include Risperdal, Seroquel, Zyprexa, Geodon, and Abilify. Although the side effects from the newer medications are considered to be less extreme, these are powerful medications that require careful management by skilled psychiatrists. As with most psychiatric conditions, there is no exact science that will anticipate which, if any, of these medications will be most effective or have the fewest side effects. Some reports suggest that antipsychotics make HPPD worse, not better. Another study shows that antipsychotics do not help with the psychotic symptoms associated with Alzheimer's disease. Despite an imperfect track record and less-than-clear methods of action, these medicines have vastly improved the lives of millions who suffer from various forms of psychosis and schizophrenia.

The two biggest concerns around medication and the dually diagnosed are compliance and sobriety. Patients invariably at some point start to feel better or decide they are tired of the medication's side effects. If they stop taking their medication or use drugs or alcohol with the medication, symptoms of psychosis will return with a vengeance.

When dealing with co-occurring disorders, it's important to work closely with a qualified psychiatrist who is part of a treatment team. Learn about the medications, doses, and side effects. Biological intervention is critical in most instances, but it is only one part of a recovery strategy. Medication will not cure an addiction or fix the problems.

Natural Biological Interventions

Over the years, some practitioners have insisted that thought disorders are caused by malnutrition and are best treated by special diets and megavitamin therapy. While there are some anecdotal claims of success, there is no evidence to support nutritional treatment instead of medicines. Individuals who suffer from illnesses that are part of the psychotic spectrum, as well as those dealing with addiction, often have very poor eating habits and may have nutritional deficiencies. Certainly, as part of improved self-care, the general recommendations of exercise and improved diet will help.

Ongoing Psychological Evaluations

The psychological impact of impaired reality processing is profound. The effect of a psychotic episode, whether caused by drugs or mental illness, is a blend of confusion, impaired social and psychological functioning, and a sense of lingering perception that the world is no longer the same. Anyone who crosses these boundaries struggles to return to ordinary levels of thinking and functioning. As a result, psychotherapy is an absolute necessity. Not all clinicians are comfortable working with thought disturbances in addition to addiction problems. Because trust and comfort level are so important, be selective and find someone who instills confidence and clarity.

A qualified clinician can be an integral link in refining treatment strategies, ensuring treatment and medication compliance, and encouraging Twelve Step participation. As with all disorders, multidisciplinary treatment and coordination are vital. The more severe the impairment, the more comprehensive and intensive the supportive services. No single model of therapy is advocated, but a cognitive-behavioral approach and/or a dialectical behavior therapist is probably most desirable. Dialectical behavior therapy (DBT) includes dialecticism, an Eastern philosophy that is helpful for many dealing with difficult conditions. The spiritual content of DBT enhances the underpinnings of cognitive-behavioral intervention. Pragmatic, goal-oriented treatment is certainly needed.

Ongoing diagnosis of a person who's experienced psychosis is vital. Diagnoses may improve the longer the patient is sober. Conversely, if there is deterioration, the primary psychotherapist may be the first and best positioned to advocate proper changes in treatment strategy. Although patient confidentiality must be protected, it is possible to forge a clear contract with the psychological service provider so that permission is granted to notify a designated family member, sponsor, or other members of the treatment team that the patient is showing signs of impaired functioning, relapse, or atypical thinking. This delicate balance can be successfully navigated without intruding upon confidences or violating boundaries. In addition, the psychotherapist can be a key observer in calling attention to an improved clinical picture. Advocacy for reduction in medication or additional testing is often the domain of the provider of psychological services.

Interpersonal Support

Feelings of uniqueness and a tendency to isolate are symptomatic of both addiction and thought disorders. The fears, disturbed thinking, confusion, and interpersonal idiosyncrasies of someone with a psychosis may result in a tendency to avoid people.

Individuals with paranoid ideation have problems with trust, and this may result in a failure to attach to healthy supports. In addition, they are prone to peculiar dress, are sometimes fashionably defiant, and are inclined to keep conventional folks away from them. As either or both diseases progress, the degree of isolation worsens.

For some schizophrenics, mood-altering chemicals lower inhibition. One of our most disturbed patients danced and communicated with ease when high but was dysfunctional and disconnected when sober.

Current research is focused on medications that assist with negative symptoms—the flatness of emotion mentioned earlier—but the best available approach is assisting clients in the development of psychosocial skills. The need for interpersonal support is vital. Sponsors and support groups specific to thought disturbance can be of value. Finally, families will need to work on building support systems as well. A healthy family unit increases the likelihood of treatment compliance, including the building of other interpersonal supports. The family needs to encourage support building and not participate in caretaking or enabling.

Recommendations

As with mood disorders, the time from first symptom onset to clear diagnosis can take many years. When we see a patient who has a mixed presentation, we are almost hypervigilant about acquiring an accurate diagnosis as soon as possible. With co-occurring addiction and thought disturbance, especially early in the onset of either condition, we have observed many abstinent individuals become symptom-free over time. Some abstinent individuals do not get better, and for them, an aggressive course of psychiatric treatment is advised. There is evidence suggesting that the earlier an emerging psychosis is treated, the less devastating it will become. For those who have a chronic thought disturbance, working the Steps can be a bit more challenging. Additional support groups and therapies must become part of the mix. Medication adherence is also absolutely essential.

In terms of intervention, time and speed matter. Early intervention, treatment, abstinence, correct diagnosis, and support structures produce the best outcome.

Relapse rates are almost always higher with dual disorders and are almost expected. We urge quick responses in the presence of a relapse because ongoing exposure to a damaging street drug will only accelerate problems of reality impairment. Do not be seduced by this common manipulation: "I will only use alcohol (or another drug) in moderation." Any intoxicant is likely to increase damage to an already injured or vulnerable brain.

There are no absolute biological tests, nor are there absolute psychological tests. The diagnosis requires very careful behavioral observation and several forms of psychological testing. One test is not usually sufficient, nor is a brief psychiatric consultation. Objective psychological testing is very helpful but often not sufficient. Sometimes projective testing, an old and controversial art form, can, in the right hands, provide much-needed clarity. In addition, neuropsychological testing can also help sort out what is going on in terms of brain injury or health.

Be hopeful that thought disturbance symptoms will clear quickly when abstinence is achieved. Maintain that hope but do not deny reality when lingering symptoms suggest more comprehensive psychiatric and psychological care.

In some instances, we have seen way too much medication given by a diagnostician who does not consider addictive substances or their lingering effects. Practitioners not familiar with addiction and relapse may only treat the symptoms they observe. Be aware that some providers do not seriously consider that mood-altering chemicals, when used and abused by addicts, can duplicate symptoms of psychosis. Some of the medicines that help depression and/or psychosis may make certain drug-induced psychoses worse.

If your gut tells you that a diagnosis is wrong, or has been missed, do not hesitate to be assertive and ask questions. In challenging a diagnosis, you might be adding vital information that had not been considered. Getting a second opinion, especially by a professional with dual disorder expertise, may be worth your time. Also, do not hesitate to use the services of both psychologists and psychiatrists, especially those who understand addiction. Each profession has its emphasis, and one might see what the other misses.

While you do not want to see too much medication or treatment provided to a loved one who is only temporarily damaged by his or her addiction, you do want to provide necessary medication and treatment that might slow the onslaught of a serious, genetically driven thought disturbance. In either case, ongoing abstinence is absolutely vital. Here there is no ambiguity.

Case History

Malcolm held the same job for many years and rarely missed a day of work, even though he drank heavily in the evening. He was eccentric and reclusive, living alone in an apartment in Los Angeles. His friends and family loved him, despite his sometimes annoying behavior. But a few weeks after his thirty-eighth birthday, everything changed.

Malcolm was admitted to a general hospital with a severe allergic reaction to a bee sting. While waiting in the emergency room, he began detoxing from alcohol, and within a few hours, he was hallucinating and behaving erratically. He did not respond to the normal detox protocols. Instead, his hallucinations became more severe, and his behavior became threatening.

The hospital staff believed that he was experiencing a classic case of DTs (delirium tremens), the most severe form of alcohol detoxification. DTs can be life threatening if not treated aggressively. Malcolm was put into full-body restraints to protect himself and others from his violent physical reactions. His medications were increased, but strangely, he did not stop hallucinating.

He remained in full-body restraints and under heavy medication for more than a week. The hospital staff was perplexed, and the treating psychiatrist tried different medications because Malcolm was actively delusional long after the normal course of detoxification. He was also paranoid and seldom cooperative with the staff. What was the cause? If he had been in his mid-twenties, a common age of onset for schizophrenia, he would have been diagnosed and treated for schizophrenia, but this behavior made no sense for a thirty-eight-year-old.

The family gave a history of Malcolm's drinking that clearly indicated he had been an alcoholic since his twenties. But because he had graduated from college and had maintained gainful employment, everyone had looked the other way. He was sometimes erratic in his actions, and he had odd mannerisms and jokes, but he was living independently, so the alcoholism was ignored.

As Malcolm's hospital stay moved into the second week, the staff recommended that the family find a residential treatment program for alcoholism. But Malcolm's ongoing hallucinations made it impossible to place him in a chemical dependency treatment center. Even programs that were licensed for co-occurring disorders didn't have the ability to treat someone who was actively psychotic. A half-dozen interventionists were called to facilitate the transfer, but none of them would take the case because the patient was not in touch with reality.

Jeff Jay came to Los Angeles to meet with the family and hospital staff, to analyze the case, and to find a solution. After debriefing family members and friends over a period of several hours, some important facts came to the surface. It so happened that Malcolm had been in a car crash in his early twenties and sustained a serious closed-head injury. Although he was otherwise uninjured, he lost consciousness at the scene of the accident and was admitted to a hospital. He remained there for five days, until he regained the ability to walk and take care of himself.

As family and friends talked among themselves during the

debriefing, they agreed that Malcolm had never really been the same after the accident. He moved to Texas for a period of years, and when he returned to Los Angeles, he was much more reclusive and eccentric than ever. He faithfully went to work every day as a traveling tool salesman with a large geographical route, but he refused to drive at night and spent every evening in a state of extreme intoxication.

As the debriefing continued, new pieces of the puzzle came to light. Friends and family recalled that he had begun exhibiting some delusions in his late twenties. For example, he had often said that his father worked for the CIA, when in fact he was a dentist. His remarks had always been chalked up to his odd sense of humor, but perhaps he wasn't joking. It also came out that Malcolm was unable to sleep unless he drank large amounts of alcohol. If his intake was restricted, as it was once during a three-day car trip with friends on vacation, he would stay up all night and harass his friends with inane jokes, paranoid accusations, and childlike gymnastics.

Could it be that Malcolm had been suffering from schizophrenia since his twenties and that he had been masking the symptoms with alcohol? His recent hospitalization for the allergic reaction to the bee sting had been his longest period sober since college. It had immediately triggered intense hallucinations, which did not come under control until he was given antipsychotic medication on day nine. Even then, he continued with mild visual hallucinations and pervasive paranoia. The causes of schizophrenia are not known, but the illness is sometimes correlated with head trauma. Schizophrenia is a disease of adolescence or early adulthood. It was initially dismissed by the hospital staff because of Malcolm's age, but the history provided by the family called the timeline of the illness into question.

As he stabilized, Malcolm was adamant that he return home to his apartment. He made no secret of the fact that he intended to start drinking right away, although he contended that he was a very light drinker, needing only a beer or two to relax in the evening.

A modified family intervention was planned with the goal of getting Malcolm to voluntarily admit himself to a treatment center that specialized in co-occurring disorders. Many treatment centers refused the case because of his still-active hallucinations, but an appropriate facility was ultimately found.

Several of Malcolm's drinking buddies were included in the intervention, a strategy that is often avoided in typical interventions. In this case, however, they were needed to help Malcolm overcome his paranoia that his family wished to institutionalize him. They helped to provide a united front with the family that made it almost impossible for Malcolm to refuse treatment.

An intervention took place while Malcolm was still hospitalized and after the antipsychotic medication had begun to alleviate his symptoms. The intervention included hospital staff, family members from three states, and longtime friends. Malcolm was moved emotionally by the love expressed in the intervention letters, and although he was still reluctant to admit he had a problem, he was willing to go to treatment to assuage the fears of the group. He went to treatment that same day.

Continued testing in the new facility verified the fact that Malcolm was schizophrenic. He ultimately responded well to a combination of antipsychotic and anticonvulsive medications. However, his road to recovery was not an easy one. He did not complete treatment the first time but instead returned to his apartment and relapsed. A secondary intervention with the threat of involuntary commitment was necessary to get him back into treatment. This time he completed primary treatment but refused the extended care that was prescribed. Again he relapsed. After a short period of time, the family intervened again, and after a brief detoxification, they were able to get him into a long-term extended care program.

Several months of clinical support were necessary to get

Malcolm to function normally on his medication. He became a regular attendee of Alcoholics Anonymous, where his quirky sense of humor was enjoyed by almost everyone. The daily routine of meetings became the backbone of his long-term recovery. Malcolm credited AA with giving him enough structure and guidance to stay on his medication and return to part-time work.

In this case, family members and friends had important information that was key to an accurate diagnosis. As puzzled as they were by the situation, they had no idea that they held the key to Malcolm's accurate diagnosis and treatment.

Another key element in Malcolm's success was that his family members didn't give up after his first treatment attempt. They kept intervening until he got all the treatment he needed to overcome his illness. Importantly, they also began their own program of recovery by attending Families Anonymous (FA) meetings. These meetings helped them to preserve their own sanity during Malcolm's trying relapses. The meetings also helped them to develop and maintain a constructive outlook. Families Anonymous provided realistic guidance based on the experience of other people who had faced similar difficulties.

When Malcolm's father passed away after a fierce battle with cancer, Malcolm had been sober five years. It was a great point of pride for Malcolm that his father had lived to see him on his feet again and not "living like a crazy man." It was also a great testimony to all the family members that they hadn't given up in the face of confusion and misdiagnosis, but had persevered until they found success.

8

Character Disorders and Addiction

What's in a name? That which we call a rose
By any other word would smell as sweet.

Romeo and Juliet (II.ii, 43–44)

Some addicts, especially more complicated addicts with multiple relapses, will get a diagnosis that falls into the character disorder or character pathology category. Character disorders are seen as deeply embedded, almost hardwired parts of personality—defects in character that are the result of early developmental problems or genetic factors. In the language of mental health professionals, these are called Axis II disorders, and they are considered difficult, sometimes impossible, to treat.

An Axis I diagnosis is something that happens to someone, most often later in life, and the event(s) may create symptoms but not alter character. For example, the death of a loved one, a divorce, or an accident may set off depression or anxiety that is problematic but does not alter character. Axis I diagnoses affect behavior, but they do not necessarily result in a permanent change of attitude or behavior at the deepest level, one's personality.

Axis II refers to long-standing, rigid patterns of thought and behavior not necessarily the result of exclusively biological or environmental events. Axis II diagnoses result in a profound change in behavior and attitudes that are enduring and resistant to treatment. An Axis II disorder may be the result of the same event—death of a parent, spouse, or pet, or perhaps a divorce—but at an earlier, more vulnerable state of development. In some instances, an event cannot be identified, and the Axis II condition is believed to be the consequence of genetics. In most instances, it is likely that both genetic sensitivity and events play a role in the onset of these disorders. Axis II disorders alter and sometimes define much of an individual's personality.

The question of personality, or character, has always been a tricky issue when talking about addiction. Before AA, most people believed that alcoholism was a result of a character problem or a personality disorder. According to the psychoanalytic line of thinking, alcoholism was the result of a developmental disorder that resulted in an oral fixation. The belief was that alcoholics were weaned prematurely or had an inadequate mothering experience that created an unmet oral dependence, later resulting in alcoholism. Although this belief was taken as fact for quite some time, clinicians no longer subscribe to this line of thinking. Nonetheless, the oral fixation idea fed right into the bias that there was something wrong with the personality or character of an addict.

Ironically, AA also includes discussion of character but in a different way. One of the tasks incorporated into a Twelve Step recovery is identifying and working on character defects. This is considered part of a healthy, fully honest reevaluation of the traits and defects that may contribute to the desire to use. The difference is that it is assumed that one is an alcoholic, regardless of personality. Decades of looking for an "alcoholic personality" have failed to identify a single personality style exclusively associated with alcoholism and addiction. Any personality style can become addicted.

Making things a bit more complex, there are some genetically vulnerable individuals who have certain behaviors and personality styles in common that are more at risk for addiction. A class of male genetic alcoholics has certain behavioral and personality features in common. They tend to become alcoholic at an early age, their disease progresses rapidly, and they are more likely to become disruptive or aggressive when intoxicated. Genetic alcoholics tend to get into a lot of difficulty, often with the law, and they eventually acquire Axis II diagnoses, including those of inter-mittent explosive personality or sociopath. For many of these ad-dicts, most or all of the character pathology disappears when they work a recovery program and stay sober.

Character, or personality, is irrelevant in predicting addiction, yet it matters in terms of treatment, attitude, and select risk fac-tors for developing the disease of addiction. This may appear to be a contradiction, but it only reinforces the fact that addictions are cunning and baffling. There is no single alcoholic personality, yet there are some common personality symptoms, or "defects," that are associated with addiction. It is also possible that the disease of addiction distorts learning, perception, and behavior, resulting in what looks like a personality or character defect that only oper-ates when the addiction is active. This particular interpretation is one that makes a lot of sense. It might be easier to understand this as we examine some of the specific character disorders, or Axis II diagnoses.

Borderline Personality Disorder

Very few diagnoses set off as strong an emotional reaction in the mental health community as borderline personality disorder (BPD). Originally, the name *borderline* referred to the transition between neurosis and psychosis. BPD is actually a disorder de-fined by emotional instability. Individuals with BPD, most often women, have problems making stable attachments with others and are prone to black-and-white thinking, self-injury, and low self-esteem. Behaviors, relationships, and emotions are highly er-ratic, and they often alienate anyone attempting to help them.

The very label of BPD can be misleading and associated with clinical failure and frustration. The real problem with BPD is the standard model of treatment: a classic, one-dimensional approach to a complicated emotional/behavioral disturbance.

BPD is, in our opinion, a misnomer for complex post-traumatic stress disorder (CPTSD), an issue we discuss in chapter 9. A growing number of clinicians object to the outdated, contaminated BPD label, and a few treatment programs do not permit the term *borderline* to be used. There is some discussion that the BPD label will be replaced by emotional dysregulation disorder (EDD), a step in the right direction. Our core objection to the term *borderline personality disorder* is all the negativity associated with it.

So what is this syndrome called borderline personality disorder that is really complex post-traumatic stress disorder but may soon be called emotional dysregulation disorder? An inability to regulate mood, extreme shifts in trust and perception, instability of relationships, self-injury, and self-loathing, coupled with anger and feelings of abandonment, are hallmarks of this particular syndrome. Those who suffer from BPD are trauma survivors, often survivors of extreme trauma at an early age. The BPD diagnosis is given about three times more often to females than to males.

Many clinicians believe that BPD is difficult to treat, but with the correct techniques and support it is quite treatable. A strong, multidimensional, coordinated approach is needed, and treating the emotional issues and the addiction at the same time is essential. Families need to find providers who understand that the core of this problem is not a developmental defect, but a complex trauma response that affects biology, interpersonal relationships, thinking, and spiritual beliefs. BPD, or CPTSD, technically fits into the category of character disorder, but we, along with some clinicians, disagree with the stigmatization and implied hopelessness of the diagnosis.

For a more complete discussion of the biological, psychological, interpersonal, and spiritual aspects of this condition, as well as treatment recommendations, review chapter 9 on post-traumatic stress disorders.

Antisocial Personality Disorder

Antisocial personality disorder (APD) is another label with negative connotations in the treatment field. APD assumes a limited conscience or absence of conscience. It is a diagnosis three times more likely to be given to males than females. Lack of empathy for others, disregard of social standards, profound self-centeredness, risk-taking behavior, lack of shame, absence of remorse, dishonesty, recklessness, aggressiveness, impulsiveness, promiscuity, a tendency to blame others, avoidance of responsibility, superficial attachments, a tendency to exploit others, and an inability to learn from prior mistakes are often cited as core features of this diagnosis.

The earlier terminology used to describe APD included "moral insanity" or "madness without delusion." In the 1800s, the term *psychopath* was coined, and it is synonymous with *sociopath.* Some refer to malignant narcissism. The language, labels, and assumptions of psychopathy are controversial and confusing. Not all people with APD are psychopaths, and not all psychopaths are criminals. Many business leaders are psychopaths, as are many politicians. They are sometimes referred to as subcriminal psychopaths or, if they are not destructive, prosocial psychopaths.

APD and Addiction

If someone fits the diagnosis of APD, the risk for addiction is increased. This is usually associated with a lack of impulse control and a desire for immediate gratification. Conversely, if you are a practicing male alcoholic and you are particularly difficult to treat, you are more likely to be given a diagnosis, or at least a tentative diagnosis, of APD. If you look at the list of characteristics that are required for the APD diagnosis, they are very similar to the behaviors and characteristics of a practicing (more often) male alcoholic. Are we dealing with a resistant addict or a personality disorder?

Another interesting consideration is this old description: The superego is alcohol soluble. This simply means that when individuals consume alcohol, all inhibitions associated with restraint and moral conscience (superego) disappear. We cannot see a superego on a scan or X-ray; it is a descriptive concept, but it appears to be grounded in emerging brain science. It will be interesting to see how current imaging technology will clarify our understanding of this description.

Biological Aspects

Biological aspects are often considered core causes of this condition. Because APD traits often run in family lines, it is believed by many that APD is the product of a neurobiological and genetic anomaly. Environmental factors can elicit identical characteristics, and males, who tend to act out their frustrations, may act in ways that are identical to genetically determined APD patients. There is also a possibility that trauma survivors, who have a restricted range of emotional expression and a history of conduct disorder, may incorrectly be given this label. A restricted range of emotional expression is a common factor in addiction, CPTSD, and APD. These common threads result in confusion for clinicians and clients. If determined solely by genetics, psychotherapeutic approaches would be ineffective. However, if caused by traumatic events, abuse, or neglect, treatment can work.

Psychological Aspects

With APD, perceptions are considered distorted but not psychotic. Individuals with APD tend to write their own rules of conduct, morality, and reality. Perhaps the easiest way to understand the psychology involved in APD is to articulate what is known as the narcissistic core of APD. Essentially, narcissism is fueled by a tendency to "twist reality to fit your convenience." Individuals with APD operate on this theme, and they also tend to ignore standard social values, are in opposition to them, or just fail to perceive them.

Interpersonal Aspects

With APD, relationships are casual, superficial, and oriented toward getting one's immediate needs met. Individuals with APD have difficulty with loyalty, honesty, and attachment. However, they appear sincere and tend to manipulate others on the basis of their pseudo-sincerity. It has been said that good psychopaths can pick your pocket, get caught, and then charm you to the point where you thank them for selecting you. There is some argument as to whether people with APD experience feelings or are skilled at turning them off, a process known as dissociation. It may well be that the degree to which feelings are processed or "turned off" may be connected to how much of the APD syndrome is genetically "wired in" versus acquired through trauma or the addiction process.

Spiritual Aspects

Although many individuals with APD appear to be spiritual, they tend to operate with a narcissistic core. In fact, some spiritual leaders use their interpersonal duplicity to prey upon the vulnerability of others. Finding a true spiritual core, if actually achieved, appears to be a real factor in healing and sustained behavioral change.

Treatment

To some extent, traditional addiction treatment programs work well with those who have APD features but may not meet the diagnostic criteria for full character pathology. There are a number of treatment programs designed for individuals with APD. These tend to use the boot camp approach. These programs work on the principle that some patients need harsh consequences if treatment professionals are to get their attention. If a patient leaves her coffee cup on the table, for example, she must wear it around her neck all day. Or if other patients use inappropriate language or show disrespect, they might get their heads shaved. While it may be appropriate and helpful for some individuals, this approach can be extremely harmful for those who have been abused and only appear to have APD. Trauma-based symptoms are treatable but by completely different methods. A young male who is really a trauma survivor, not an APD, will be further traumatized and feel abused by these powerful techniques.

Clinicians have long observed a pattern of burnout for APD. Many young people display conduct disorders into young adulthood but then mysteriously start to mellow in their late twenties. This phenomenon is believed to be the result of a slow maturation process. The APD patient's conscience is believed to be slow to develop. Not everyone experiences this burnout; many individuals continue to engage in manipulative and antisocial behaviors throughout their lives.

Histrionic Personality Disorder

Histrionic personality disorder (HPD) is associated with highly dramatic and theatrical displays of behavior, and it is a diagnosis far more frequently given to women. Individuals with this disorder seek attention, are lacking in insight, are selectively disconnected from certain emotions, and can overreact to seemingly insignificant issues. They are manipulative, but, unlike persons with APD or sociopathy, they are unaware of their manipulations. This lack of awareness and insight is a core characteristic of HPD. They can be highly flirtatious, demanding, irritable, and irrational, although they are also superficially charming. Individuals with HPD are easily influenced by others, tend to become involved emotionally with males who suffer from APD, lack empathy for others, are extremely self-centered, and are highly focused on outward appearances. These individuals tend to have multiple physical complaints, often exaggerated and self-medicated. It is believed that they convert their emotional conflicts into exaggerated but often vague physical symptoms. They are highly dependent upon others yet have difficulty with meaningful relationships. They are insecure but tend to deny it. Superficial, detached, and vain, HPD individuals are considered to have less than fully developed personalities.

In some respects, this is similar to BPD, but with HPD the emphasis is upon a more theatrical style and one that is often associated with neurotic issues, including multiple, exaggerated physical complaints. There is also a core of narcissism in that these individuals feel they are always correct, never at fault. They are eager to please but can become impulsive and angry without warning.

Individuals with HPD tend to have boundary issues. They are flirtatious, but they are not always aware of it. The disconnection between behavior, intent, and conscious choice is a hallmark of HPD. Because of their inner emptiness and multiple physical discomforts, individuals with HPD are highly vulnerable to addictive disorders. They tend to gravitate toward opiates, benzodiazepines, and alcohol. They may have legitimate medical issues, but these issues tend to be exaggerated to gain attention and/or mood-altering chemicals. Those who have HPD tend to be immature and do not think about inner issues.

Seemingly compliant, those who have HPD can be difficult to treat. They sabotage treatment, create crises, and easily feel betrayed and abandoned. They thrive on crisis and seek out exciting, powerful others to satisfy their own inner emptiness. Despite their desire to please, they can be difficult to engage in treatment because they seek quick fixes and avoid complex emotions. The key to treating individuals given HPD diagnoses is to slow them down, engage them in a journey of self-discovery, encourage them to avoid superficial relationships, and forge a therapeutic alliance where they can get accurate feedback about behaviors and issues they would prefer not to see. The denial that most addicts bring to treatment is far more extensive with individuals diagnosed with HPD. Be aware of what is called a "flight into health," essentially a declared quick fix that is intended to shorten treatment or undermine sustained adherence to recovery recommendations. These individuals tend to need more time and structure before they get it. They tend to be very vulnerable to relationship addiction and sexual addiction, and they must be strongly encouraged to stay away from seeking out or responding to exciting but immature relationships that are doomed to fail.

These individuals respond well to individual therapy, such as cognitive-behavioral therapy with a more insight-oriented focus. They may also need to build pain management skills, and they may need treatment for other issues, such as depression.

In our opinion, the HPD diagnosis is a variant of the BPD diagnosis and may be part of what should be relabeled emotional dysregulation disorder. Also, as with BPD, there is often a history of trauma associated with this disorder.

Narcissistic Personality Disorder

Narcissism is the valuing or loving of one's self. A moderate amount of narcissism is considered healthy and represents a balance of care between others and self. Too little narcissism, and we are likely to suffer from anxiety or feelings of inferiority. Pathological narcissism—a personality style, not a formal diagnosis—is when one's own needs consistently supersede the needs of others, to the detriment of others. A narcissistic personality disorder (NPD) is even more extreme: An individual diagnosed with NPD has almost no capacity for empathy and tends to see things only from a narrow, self-serving perspective.

Patients with NPD tend to avoid treatment. They do not see or accept the possibility of an internal flaw. Anything that goes wrong is someone else's fault, not their own. They can twist communications, recollections, and perceptions to suit their own interests. In fact, one of the more succinct descriptions of pathological narcissism is "the ability to twist reality to suit one's convenience." People with NPD are not necessarily antisocial. Many highly accomplished and prosocial individuals function at the highest levels of society. A common problem is the inability to forge lasting, reciprocal, and balanced primary relationships. While there is usually no malevolence involved, interpersonal dynamics in relationships are essentially one-sided, and conciliation or empathy is not usually available. Individuals with NPD do not see anything wrong with their behaviors. They tend to comply at a superficial level, resist input from others, and seek control. This sounds like many resistant addicts, and, in fact, a narcissistic style of functioning is very frequently observed with addicts who are not yet in recovery. Although there is no "alcoholic personality," psychological tests consistently show elevated degrees of narcissism as addicts begin treatment and an observable and significant drop if they proceed through treatment successfully. Some observers suggest that Twelve Step programs are the most effective form of treatment for those with a narcissistic personality style, some of whom may meet the technical criteria for NPD.

Conversely, it is possible that the process of addiction is dependent upon a foundation of narcissism. If, as brain scientists are now conceptualizing, addiction is a brain disorder that distorts learning and perception, one of the main areas of impact may be in the realm we call narcissism. It is possible that denial, a classic feature of addicts, is actually a form of narcissism where reality is twisted to fit a distorted, self-serving agenda.

The cause of NPD is not clear, but a high degree of genetic loading is assumed. However, there are many who believe that NPD can only develop if there is a strong sense of inferiority during early development. Whether the addiction process contributes to NPD or people prone to NPD are more vulnerable to addiction is not clear. Although a formal NPD diagnosis is not common in co-occurring disorders (other symptoms may obscure NPD or a narcissistic personality style), some degree of narcissistic dysfunction is often ascribed to addicts in early treatment.

Treatment

Individual psychotherapy is not considered highly effective in treating NPD, but coupled with a Twelve Step program, the individual focus and accurate feedback may help provide additional guidance that will make a difference. Individuals who have NPD and a co-occurring addiction need accurate, impartial behavioral feedback, but they also need support and judicious validation.

This delicate balance may be facilitated by adding a psychotherapy professional, but one who is very savvy with addictive disorders. Biological interventions are not common unless there are other disturbances. There are no psychiatric medicines, other than accurate feedback, that can be given to someone with NPD and a co-occurring addiction. It is possible that these individuals may be responsive to anticraving and mood-stabilizing medication, but this is not connected to the narcissistic disorder.

Paranoid Personality Disorder

Paranoid personality disorders (PPDs)are characterized by a sustained sense of threat, a sense of doom due to the malice of others, a perception of uniqueness, and feelings of being victimized by others. Different from paranoid ideation, paranoid schizophrenia, and paranoia associated with certain drugs such as methamphetamine or hallucinogens, PPD characteristics include a fear-based view of the world that does not necessarily include psychotic features. There are distortions of perception and peculiar belief systems, but there is often a lack of a fully developed psychosis.

Individuals with PPD avoid attachments because of their ongoing fear of betrayal. They may be argumentative, detached, and hostile. They are meticulously private and can become aggressive when they feel threatened. PPD patients often avoid mood-altering chemicals because they fear others and fear losing control. However, paranoid thinking—some of it extreme— is often observed with active addicts or those damaged by specific drugs. A drug-induced paranoia is different from PPD. The general assumption is that PPD would precede the use of mood-altering chemicals. Individuals with PPD who become addicts are highly vulnerable to becoming psychotic over time, secondary to the damage of alcohol or another drug of choice.

As with all personality disorders, it is assumed there is a high genetic loading or an early developmental disturbance, such as abuse or neglect.

Schizoid Personality Disorder

Often mistaken for schizotypal personality disorder (discussed below), those with schizoid personality disorder have core problems in forming relationships. They are highly isolated and fear close relationships. They feel inadequate and avoid interpersonal commitments. Their interpersonal style is flat, awkward, and wooden. They seem odd, detached, and disconnected. They engage in dissociation almost all the time. Although they may distort perceptions, as we observed with narcissism, patients with schizoid personality disorder do not have psychotic episodes.

The schizoid personality is believed to be connected to early attachment failures. In analytic literature, this is attributed to an anxious or neglectful mother. An alternative position is that this disorder is genetically similar to the asocial and disconnected style observed with Asperger's syndrome, a mild form of autism. Finally, some trauma survivors whose baseline style is dissociative may mistakenly receive a schizoid personality disorder diagnosis.

Individuals with schizoid personality disorder have a desire to numb feelings and tend to be attracted to alcohol and benzodiazepines. This diagnosis is less common than other Axis II disorders in co-occurring treatment settings. Because almost all addiction recovery involves building of therapeutic relationships, this can be a tricky co-occurring disorder. Invariably, an individual psychotherapy approach is needed, but it must also be tied to an expectation of active participation in abstinence-based recovery. Medicines are not usually prescribed unless there is an additional problem such as an anxiety disorder or depression.

Schizotypal Personality Disorder

Patients with schizotypal personality disorder tend to display the negative symptoms associated with psychotic disorders. These individuals behave oddly. They look unusual and act differently because they respond to a different set of interpersonal and social cues. They may have psychotic episodes, but these are not necessarily sustained. Many consider the schizotypal personality disorder to be a precursor to or a resting state between psychotic episodes. Individuals with this disorder tend to have distorted perceptions of themselves or others, but for the most part, they do not experience active hallucinations. People with schizotypal personality disorders may have paranoid beliefs, but they are not full-blown paranoid schizophrenics. Nor do they fit the diagnosis of PPD. A peculiar interpersonal style seems to be the hallmark of this disorder. Individuals who fit this diagnosis are at high risk for psychotic breaks, or a breakdown of reality. They are also likely to abuse and become addicted to chemicals.

A schizotypal personality disorder diagnosis is often given to younger, atypical individuals, more often males, who have prepsychotic symptoms. They isolate, think in an idiosyncratic, asocial fashion, and may be prone to nonproductive rumination. They seem to take pride in appearing separate, yet they often detach themselves from the counterculture they appear to emulate. This is a serious diagnosis and, if correct, is associated with significant levels of dysfunction, asocial behavior, addiction, and homelessness. Our remarks about etiology and treatment for schizophrenia are applicable. It is urgent to get these individuals sober and interrupt the additional damage done by the disease of addiction. These individuals are treatable; aggressive treatment with appropriate medication, coupled with structure and psychological care, can result in good outcomes.

Avoidant, Dependent, and Obsessive-Compulsive Disorders

These diagnoses are referred to as the fear-based cluster of personality disorders. These diagnoses have considerable overlap with anxiety disorders, phobias, and social phobias. They describe specific styles of coping that seem to be connected to the fear of criticism from others. Not surprisingly, the avoidant personality separates and detaches from social situations. Dependent personalities rely completely on others in decision making, are terrified of being alone, and avoid forming or articulating their own judgments. Obsessive-compulsive individuals engage in excessive worry, ritualized behaviors, and a quest for perfect order. They can be rigid, guarded, controlling, and inflexible.

Biopsychosocial Overview

Although there are distinct clusters of personality disorders (odd, erratic, or fear-based), they all have some common features. These diagnoses imply a powerful level of dysfunction and are associated with poor response to treatment. In terms of the biological aspects, most of these diagnoses are deeply wired patterns that most likely have specific, but yet unknown, genetic and brain dysfunction features. Defects in perception, reality processing, attachments, social functioning, emotional processing, and personality balance are possible consequences of these disorders. Alternatively, early exposure to traumatic or catastrophic levels of stress can result in the same diagnosis. The degree of psychological disruption, as well as interpersonal disruption, is significant.

One fact we would like to emphasize is that extreme trauma, even later in life, can result in symptoms that are identical to character pathology. Although biology and early development are most commonly noted, stress alone later in life can result in very similar or identical symptoms.

Regardless of causation, those who fit the character pathology description are definitely treatable, although their treatment requires more time and effort.

Summary

Character pathology is a way of describing core areas of dysfunction that are considered problems at a personality level. This separate category is called Axis II and is distinguished from the less deeply embedded conditions in Axis I. What makes personality disorders unique is that they are relatively enduring features of function that are very deeply woven into all areas of behavior and perception. Character pathology assumes a greater degree of permanence at all levels: interpersonal behavior, perception, and emotional regulation. We see large numbers of complex female addicts diagnosed with borderline personality disorder, a label whose validity we question, and more males diagnosed with anti-social personality disorder, a confusing and often inaccurate label for those struggling with co-occurring disorders.

There is no such thing as a singular alcoholic personality, yet there are certain personality styles and characteristics that are associated with higher risk for addiction. Whether character path-ology causes addiction or addiction causes character pathology is unclear, yet many people are quick to make premature and in-accurate assumptions. In either case, the diagnosis of a personality disorder is a powerful event that impacts everyone's perception of the individual.

When is a difficult individual declared character disordered? Where exactly is the line drawn? When do patients cross the line into this other world—Axis II, or character pathology? We have observed many Axis II disorders disappear as soon as the indi-vidual is sober. This tells us that either the diagnosis was wrong or that addiction, coupled with certain personality features or heavy trauma, will mimic character pathology. Then again, many indi-viduals get sober and appear to continue acting in ways that fit the descriptions of character pathology. This group is more vulnerable to relapse, but many stay sober for the remainder of their lives.

Quite simply, a character pathology label tells us that the sever-ity level is likely above average and relapse risks are likely higher. The diagnosis alone does not tell us how to proceed; it simply tells us we need to be prepared for greater challenges. It may also give us some information about personality style. That is far different from the implied and sometimes declared hopelessness too often attached to the Axis II, or character pathology, tradition.

Recommendations

If a diagnosis of character pathology is given to your loved one, be prepared for a more complex set of issues, possibly requiring more time, structure, accountability, and Step work. Clever addicts sometimes revel in the cloud of confusion created in families after an Axis II diagnosis. Sometimes the Axis II diagnosis results in families losing hope and balance. We have seen too many families give up or go to extremes of tough love when this label is used. More effort, better boundaries, and greater determination are required, not rigidity. Families need to be firm *and* loving, not one to the exclusion of the other.

We have observed these diagnoses given prematurely or inaccurately, so families might wish to seek a second opinion. Subsequent to being given an Axis II diagnosis, if families find that the provider, facility, or institution has adopted a negative attitude toward their loved one, or toward the client population overall, they may wish to seek other providers.

We advocate an attitude of hopefulness and an assumption that the patient can and will heal. The attitude of the patient and of the provider is perhaps the best predictor of therapeutic success. We prefer the AA tradition of encouraging work on character defects. This is particularly relevant in more severe cases. Working on character defects as part of recovery, and working intensively with mental health professionals to address deeply rooted injuries or biologically driven perceptual flaws, is certainly the goal of a good recovery plan. Many individuals with character disorders get better as soon as they are sober. Many disorders burn out spontaneously when biology matures. Other persons find ways of redirecting their character defects in a prosocial rather than an antisocial or self-destructive manner. Intensive psychotherapy in addition to committed Step work can have startling results.

Case History

Sean's parents dreaded their meeting with the psychiatrist. Their twenty-seven-year-old son had been in treatment several times for alcoholism and drug addiction, and now he was locked in an urban psychiatric facility. He had recently been arrested for breaking and entering and had become violent with the police. When he started detoxing in jail, he was transferred to the hospital, and when he resisted treatment, he was placed in the locked ward.

Sean had grown up in a solid, middle-class neighborhood with a large extended family. He was athletic and popular in high school but given to risky behavior. His minor run-ins with the law were discounted by his parents as a youthful phase. He was so charming and gregarious that few people doubted his ultimate success in the world.

But shortly after high school, Sean began using cocaine along with alcohol. He was already a daily drinker, and he now became a daily user of the expensive white powder as well. He had no way to finance this expensive habit, and so he began selling small amounts to friends and acquaintances that he met in nightclubs and bars.

In the years that followed, Sean crashed several cars, was arrested for cocaine possession, and left a trail of angry girlfriends. He went through three outpatient programs and two residential treatment programs, always promising to turn himself around but never lasting more than a week or two in the real world. Through it all, he exuded a sense of optimism and self-confidence that lulled both his counselors and his parents into a hopeful trance. In fact, he was highly manipulative and always used treatment to avoid legal consequences.

But as his addiction worsened and his need for money grew, he started down the path of a petty criminal. As his associates sank lower on the social scale, so, too, did his ways and means of getting money. His parents refused to help him, in the hope that he would "hit bottom," but now he was in serious trouble. He had been arrested and had started a fight with the police. He seemed to become psychotic, so the officers brought him to the psychiatric facility. His parents now awaited the diagnosis of the doctor with a sense of foreboding.

"I have to be frank with you," said the psychiatrist, looking up from Sean's chart. "There is little hope for your son. I have seen this too many times before."

"But he's only twenty-seven," said his mother. "Surely there must be something you can do to help him."

"Your son has had five previous treatment attempts, and he has made no progress. He doesn't care what he does, and he doesn't care who he hurts," said the doctor. "He is an impulse-ridden sociopath, addicted to cocaine and alcohol, and when he gets out of jail or prison, he will go right back to his old ways. His chances of recovery are less than one in a hundred."

"But what are we to do?" asked his father.

"Pray," said the doctor, closing the file. "We have good treatments for addiction, and your son has been exposed to them. But there is no treatment for the kind of antisocial personality disorder that Sean has demonstrated over the last few years."

"Antisocial what?" said his mother.

"Your son is suffering from antisocial personality disorder, and it is not treatable with medication or talk therapy. He has little or no conscience, and he has no loyalty to anyone or anything but his own desires. He will do whatever it takes to feed his demons."

"But . . ."

"Pray that some change comes over him or that he somehow grows out of it," said the psychiatrist. "Those are the only ways I have ever seen a positive resolution to such cases. It will also help to keep him in treatment, if he'll accept it, because it's a better incubator for miracles than a jail cell."

Sean was eager to trade treatment for jail at his upcoming court date, and the judge agreed to a two-year program in a boot-camp-style facility. Sean knew he was getting close to a prison sentence, and he wanted to avoid that at all costs.

Over the course of many months, Sean became acclimated to being alcohol and drug free. For the first time in years, his brain was completely free of mood-altering chemicals for an extended period. By the time he reached eighteen months of enforced sobriety, he was beginning to think differently. Many of the other men in the boot camp had been to prison, and Sean could see that he was headed there too, if he didn't make a change in his life. It was pure self-preservation and self-interest that motivated him to start asking for help.

Gradually, he began working in earnest with his counselors and participating more honestly in the mandatory AA meetings. He became convinced that this was his last chance, and he was desperate to find a solution. He read, he talked, and he listened. Over time, he began to develop a little faith.

Luckily for Sean, his antisocial personality disorder (APD) was not set in stone. Sometimes addiction and its many symptoms can masquerade as a personality disorder, and in this case it may be that Sean's relentless urge to use alcohol and drugs made him look like he was suffering from APD. However, his involuntary sobriety, his long residential treatment experience, and other unseen forces worked together to change the dynamics of his life. When he was released from the boot camp program, he continued with his AA meetings, never missing a day. He got a sales job at which he excelled, and he avoided transitory relationships.

Things did not go smoothly for Sean, but he did not relapse in the face of problems. He worked closely with an AA sponsor and stuck with the one-day-at-a-time philosophy. It appeared that Sean had a spiritual awakening during his long treatment experience. He did not become overtly religious, but he made a decision to follow the program of Alcoholics Anonymous to the letter.

Sean had heard the same description from the psychiatrist that his parents did: "an impulse-ridden sociopath." Sean now admits that the doctor was probably right, but fortunately that wasn't the end of the story. The judge did Sean a great favor by mandating a long-term treatment program. It allowed him the time necessary to regain control of his life.

Sean has been clean and sober now for many years and has recently opened his own business, based on his old sales job. He continues to follow a program of recovery and is adamant about the need for recovering people to find a Higher Power.

"As long as I was calling the shots," says Sean, "I always got myself into trouble. I was crazy and I just couldn't help myself. But I finally came to believe that a Power greater than myself could restore me to sanity. I made a decision to follow that path. And that has made all the difference."

9

Post-traumatic Stress Disorder, Complex Post-traumatic Stress Disorder, and Addiction

Ever since my eight-year-old daughter's death in 1993, I have been drinking to kill the pain. I know that I am an alcoholic— but I am one only because of this tragedy. That one day changed my life and made me what I am today.

Elizabeth, age 47, recovering alcoholic

The idea that traumatic events cause addiction has been around for centuries, and studies show that addiction rates increase for people who have been in active combat, have endured physical or sexual abuse, have witnessed a murder, or have been personally involved in other unbearably stressful situations or events. At the same time, addictions occur without being preceded by a trauma, and traumas occur without addiction as a consequence. It should also be noted that individuals who become addicts are more likely to experience traumatic consequences; violence, accidents, and illness are often the result of an addictive disorder. While a connection between trauma and addiction is indisputable, the causality is not so simple. Although we may be somewhat biased, we believe that trauma is the most important and long-neglected link between addiction and co-occurring disorders.

Most traumatic events affect people for a short period of time. Acute episodes of depression or anxiety might follow a significant loss, accident, or assault. The vast majority of stressful and even traumatic events resolve naturally, without professional assistance or lasting symptoms. When traumatic events have a lasting impact on a person, over a period of more than six months, then one of the two most disruptive trauma disorders may result— post-traumatic stress disorder (PTSD) or complex post-traumatic stress disorder (CPTSD).

Post-traumatic stress disorder is an anxiety disorder with symptoms that include intrusive thoughts, intense emotions, lasting fear, avoidance of certain stimuli, and lasting biological changes, such as hypervigilance. Complex post-traumatic stress disorder is not listed in the current *DSM IV-TR* but is recognized by trauma experts as the more extreme form of the same condition. CPTSD may involve more intense trauma, more frequent trauma, and an earlier age of exposure to the first trauma. Individuals with CPTSD have symptoms of such intrusive power that their entire attitude, and perhaps personality, is altered as a result of trauma.

Following are some brief facts about the association of trauma disorders and addiction:

+ Approximately 25 to 33 percent of alcoholics and addicts have or have had significant PTSD.
+ It is estimated that 25 percent of those exposed to a trauma will develop either PTSD or CPTSD. Whether a trauma disorder develops and what type varies according to the type of trauma (random or man-made), frequency, intensity, age of exposure to it, and other factors.
+ Trauma-related symptoms can increase the odds for developing an addiction.
+ Up to 80 percent of those with active PTSD have substance abuse problems, and many of them cross the line into addiction.
+ Being an addict or an alcoholic greatly increases the chances of having a trauma disorder.

+ PTSD and CPTSD change how the brain works.
+ Addicts and alcoholics who have a trauma disorder tend to have CPTSD.
+ Treatments that work for PTSD can make CPTSD worse.
+ The addiction must be treated first.
+ Treatment for CPTSD must begin as soon as possible after getting sober because addiction relapse is likely within six months.

Most people are somewhat familiar with PTSD, a disorder that clinicians first identified with soldiers but quickly expanded to include a wide range of unmanageable life events and circumstances. The sustained symptoms altered the way we interpret the consequences of trauma. Early experts referred to this disorder as shell shock, operational fatigue, battle fatigue, and war neurosis. A new label, PTSD, entered our vocabulary after the Vietnam War.

PTSD and CPTSD can be further defined as

1. *A normal set of reactions to abnormal events.* One reason this definition is so powerful is that it puts almost complete emphasis on the impact of events on the person, not the inherent defect in personality or development. Although not a complete definition, it is a clinically useful and simple way of describing what happens. This viewpoint is similar to addicts looking at their addiction as a disease. Addiction and PTSD happen to a person but do not reflect a lack of strength of moral fiber. Most addicts begin to heal when they hear and accept the concept that their symptoms are not their fault. Similarly, survivors of trauma need to hear that they are not inadequate failures. By normalizing PTSD and CPTSD, we set the healing process in motion.

2. *A chronic and phasic condition.* Trauma disorders can be treated effectively but are chronic conditions—there is no cure. They are also phasic, or come and go. Symptoms reappear, most often with a specific trigger or anniversary. PTSD and CPTSD are only diagnosed if, six months after the trauma, symptoms persist. In many cases, people experience a delay of onset—they do not have symptoms for months, years, and even decades after the trauma. Many survivors of childhood sexual abuse, for example, do not have symptoms until they reach their childbearing years. Many soldiers will be fine for several years and then develop symptoms.

3. *Producing symptoms in all major areas of functioning.* PTSD and CPTSD disrupt thinking, mood stability, spirituality, and interpersonal relationships. CPTSD, in particular, results in deep and profound impact in all of these major areas of functioning.

Developing PTSD or CPTSD

Trauma disorders begin when people experience or witness an event that makes them feel powerless and overwhelmed. Most of us experience tragic loss, helplessness, and overload, but not everyone develops lasting symptoms. About 25 percent of those who go through traumatic event(s) develop symptoms. Why the other 75 percent do not develop symptoms is unknown, but it is not simply a function of willpower or personality.

The following are some factors that increase the likelihood that a person will develop PTSD or CPTSD symptoms:

1. Age. The younger a person is when exposed to a traumatic event, the more likely she will be affected.

2. Events that involve human-to-human harm, injury, negligence, or malice. (Natural disasters are less likely to produce symptoms.)

3. Events that are intense, that are stressful for a long time (such as a kidnapping or being a prisoner of war), or that happen repeatedly (such as sexual abuse by a parent).
4. Being blamed for the event.
5. Lack of a solid support system. Being part of a group appears to provide some protection from developing psychological and physical conditions.
6. Lack of training in how to handle anticipated stressors, or underdeveloped coping skills. Specific conditioning and training can reduce the likelihood of trauma disorder. People in high-risk jobs undergo specific training to help them master emotions and transcend danger.
7. Poor leadership during a crisis. Combat units with poor leadership have a higher psychiatric casualty rate than units in comparable situations with strong leadership.

Biological Aspects

Trauma disorders change brain biology and brain biochemistry. The changes may be temporary for acute stress, but if the symptoms persist beyond a month, permanent changes are likely. Stressful situations set off a series of alarms resulting in huge hormonal and neurobiological changes that prepare us for survival—fight or flight or the drive to protect or nurture. The cascade of changes that stress sets off usually quiets down as soon as the threat abates. Natural healing occurs when a state of balance resumes. If the balancing mechanisms fail or the perceived or actual stress continues, we have conditions that would produce symptoms of PTSD or CPTSD.

The ongoing alarm mechanism associated with PTSD appears to damage the primitive part of the brain known as the limbic system. The limbic system includes the amygdala, a part of the brain that, when stimulated, makes us fearful. The hippocampus, which coordinates primitive and advanced parts of the brain, appears to incur cellular damage. With a trauma disorder, the limbic system stays on high alert, while the neocortex, the advanced, thinking, objective, analytic part of the brain, shuts off. Fear takes over almost completely. This is very similar to the hijacked brain idea used to describe addiction. With PTSD and addiction, objective reasoning appears to stop. Primitive impulses overrule the higher, reasoning parts of the brain. There are differences in terms of perception and pathways, but PTSD, CPTSD, and addiction turn off our ability to reason. This is why we cannot readily reason with someone in a state of panic or acute intoxication. This biological shift from higher reasoning to primitive reasoning is a major part of what happens as a result of trauma.

With a trauma disorder, primitive thinking can overrule logic whenever fear is stimulated, a process known as triggering. A person can be logical one moment, but if triggered by a smell associated with a trauma, for example, the person relives the event and loses touch with current circumstances. The alarms go off, reasoning stops, and feelings of dread, anger, and volatility take over. We may be stunned to see a loved one transform from rational to hyperemotional, angry, fearful, or distant. The biological process is rapid and powerful. What is really happening is the higher level of intellect, grounded in the present, is suddenly abducted, or hijacked, by the primitive part of the brain. Those who have PTSD or CPTSD tend to live in a chronic state of emotional arousal, and triggering events bring intense reactions not observed in individuals without this diagnosis.

People who have trauma disorders go through a fundamental change in how they perceive the world and react to additional stress. On the one hand, they tend to avoid getting triggered. This avoidance sometimes includes a phenomenon known as *dissociation*, or a detached state. When dissociated, patients can come across as cold and detached toward loved ones. On the other hand, when they are triggered, they become more sensitive to stress; they feel more easily threatened, they feel more anxious, and they are often more vulnerable to depression. The core problem of PTSD and CPTSD may be the inability to moderate or balance emotion. In other words, after a trauma, the symptomatic person is more likely to be overreactive or underreactive. They are commonly described as having a hot-and-cold emotional style or a black-and-white worldview. This inability to moderate emotions, technically called *affective dysregulation*, is the same process we observe with mood disorders. In fact, bipolar disorders have a great deal in common with PTSD and CPTSD. Alcohol and other mood-altering drugs may also damage the circuits that provide balance and emotional moderation. Trauma, addiction, and mood disorders share many common features.

Another interesting biological consequence of stress disorders is the apparent connection with certain physical conditions. Those who have suffered childhood sexual abuse, for example, seem to be at much higher risk for fibromyalgia, reflex sympathetic dystrophy (RSD), chronic fatigue syndrome, migraines, lower back pain, and certain digestive disorders. It is believed that the ongoing strain on the immune system increases the frequency of some of these conditions.

Psychological Aspects

Individuals who develop trauma disorders think differently than they did before the trauma. Sometimes referred to as victim thinking, the tendency is to personalize many things that might be overlooked by a nontraumatized person. Heightened levels of shame, self-blame, and guilt are also commonly observed. This self-loathing feeds into a phenomenon that we refer to as repetitive and compulsive self-invalidating behavior. The victim part of the psyche is self-destructive, and the addict part of the psyche seeks relief from the self-destructive thoughts and other symptoms. One disorder perpetuates the other, and the addict engages in a slow suicide. This dynamic is rather pronounced when accompanied by trauma disorders, particularly CPTSD.

Those who have PTSD or CPTSD tend to have a constricted range of emotional expression and, often, limited empathy. They have difficulty with emotional subtlety. They might overreact to the death of a small animal, yet show no reaction to a news report about a murder or rape. They tend to be distracted by the multiple thoughts they juggle. This split consciousness, part of the complex phenomenon of dissociation, is nothing bizarre or mystical. All people dissociate to a certain degree. If we drive a car, listen to the radio, and talk on a cell phone at the same time, we are dissociating. Our cognitive efficiency drops, and the likelihood of an accident increases.

Survivors learn to split awareness following a trauma. They think obsessively about what went wrong and what they failed to do, and then they try to pay attention to what is going on in real time. This dissociation is natural immediately after a trauma, but if this thought process continues at least six months after the event, the survivor is considered to have PTSD or CPTSD. It may be a constant phenomenon on a quasiconscious level, but it does become heightened following a trigger exposure. Many survivors have three, four, or even five streams of thought going on at the same time. It is little wonder that those who suffer from PTSD and CPTSD seem preoccupied, distracted, and distant. Dissociation creates an overload in cognition, known as cognitive intrusion, that disrupts efficiency and affects relationships. The more severe the disturbance, the more pronounced the cognitive intrusion.

Interpersonal Aspects

Those who develop PTSD or CPTSD tend to isolate. They suffer from simultaneous arrogance and shame. The shame is based upon blame for failing to control the uncontrollable. The arrogance is based on feelings of uniqueness. They think, *Ordinary folks who have not been through really rough times cannot relate to me and are beneath me. How can I trust somebody whose main trauma was a parking ticket?* This combination of arrogance and shame results in interpersonal silence and failure to participate in ordinary relationships. PTSD and CPTSD sufferers trust very few people and tend to consider only other survivors as trustworthy. Individuals with active symptoms of PTSD, and especially CPTSD, do not form the deep attachments that can help them get healthy and get through ordinary and extraordinary life stressors. Most are unaware of the role they play in keeping people at bay.

Spiritual Aspects

Many trauma survivors struggle overtly or covertly with beliefs of fairness. They question how a Higher Power could have abandoned them. In addition, they wonder why they themselves could not function to do the impossible. Individuals with PTSD or CPTSD have problems accepting their imperfections as well as accepting the disappointment of the spiritual system of their backgrounds. Although many survivors have strong spiritual intuition, their feelings of abandonment often turn to cynicism, and many individuals report a feeling of inner emptiness: "It feels like I have a hole in my chest or a hole in my spirit." This is not different from what many alcoholics report, but it does tend to be more emphatic and disruptive with co-occurring trauma disorders.

People who have CPTSD tend to be more than cynical. They tend to be nihilistic. Nihilism refers to a belief system that is without hope or a sense of a positive future. Individuals with CPTSD have such intense negativity that they feel it important to prove their worldview over and over. They behave in ways that almost guarantee rejection as a way to prove what they so firmly believe.

Trauma Disorders and Addiction

The onset of a trauma disorder can occur before, during, or after the onset of an addictive disorder. Many people like to think of it happening in a linear fashion—trauma occurs, self-medication follows, and addiction results. In fact, it can be the other way around. We can be raised in a sane, loving, and stable family environment, then we start using, become addicted, and suffer extremely traumatic consequences. Addiction is associated with numerous consequences, including accidents, violence, and rape.

Both addictive disorders and trauma disorders involve a dominant limbic system, the part of the brain that controls instinct. The limbic message for a trauma survivor demands safety, often including isolation and anger. The addict may desire recreation, amusement, or numbing. The neurological pathways may differ, but the issue of limbic system dominance seems to be involved with both conditions.

Drug users and those who've suffered a trauma may at some point cross an invisible line, and the learned brain pathways become hardwired. At that point, drug users are addicts and those who've suffered a trauma have a trauma disorder. Once these conditions are fully manifested, the individual cannot be cured. Even if patients stop the damaging thought patterns and behaviors, take medication for the mental illness, and abstain from alcohol and drug use, they are not cured but are in recovery.

Addiction and trauma-based disorders may mimic character disorders, or Axis II disorders. Many addicts and trauma survivors with CPTSD get inaccurately labeled as sociopaths or as having borderline personality disorder. People who have CPTSD are particularly sensitive and operate on a combination of arrogance and shame-based thinking. The term used in recovery settings is *insecure egomaniac*. Both CPTSD and addiction require self-acceptance, something that is woven into Twelve Step work and psychotherapy.

The need for stimulation and the challenges of boredom also appear to function with both addiction and trauma disorders. Many addicts seem to need more excitement than others. Referred to as sensation seeking, this impatience with the middle ground is part of what makes serenity such a challenge for many in early recovery. The need for challenges, flirting with danger, or sensation seeking is also observed with trauma survivors, especially those with CPTSD. Many addicts are also more sensitive to stress, thereby more prone to anxiety and depression. Similarly, trauma survivors experience changes on an emotional and biological level that tend to make them more anxious at times. This inner struggle between stimulation seeking and stimulation avoidance is associated with both conditions. Again, the pathways may be different, but difficulty living in the middle ground is consistent with both disorders.

Addictive disorders and trauma disorders are both affected by genetics as well as environment. The higher the genetic loading (which we estimate by looking at groups, not individuals), the more severe the symptoms. Environment also plays a role. Evidence supports the idea that the earlier an individual starts drinking, the harsher the impact. Younger brains are more readily damaged by the effects of drugs and alcohol. Similarly, the earlier the environmental exposure to trauma, the more extensive the damage.

Treating PTSD and CPTSD

As with most co-occurring disorders, treating the addiction is the first priority. The sequence of emphasis is to treat the addiction for the first thirty days and then to treat the trauma disorder and the addiction simultaneously. The idea that we can treat the trauma and that the addiction will take care of itself is unrealistic. Those who have PTSD or CPTSD and stop using after being treated for their trauma were not addicted; they had not crossed that invisible line. Old-style addiction treatment programs may recommend working on addiction only for the first year. This process does not work for those who suffer from a co-occurring trauma disorder. Left untreated, trauma symptoms are likely to cause a relapse within six months.

It is important that treatment for the co-occurring trauma

begin as soon as possible, but it should not distract from the necessary first priority: dealing with the addiction. Trauma disorders should be identified during addiction treatment but dealt with immediately after primary addiction treatment, while the individual is in early recovery and working the Steps. In an ideal world, primary treatment would deal with both disorders, but the twenty-eight-day length of stay for primary addiction treatment is just enough to establish a foundation for sobriety. As soon as that foundation is established, treatment for trauma should commence. Simultaneously working the Steps while working on trauma symptoms increases the likelihood of a good outcome. While this can often be done on an outpatient basis following primary addiction treatment, many individuals require additional supports such as extended residential treatment or halfway houses. The severity of either or both conditions will help determine the level of care.

Effective trauma treatment focuses on skill building, a conservative, symptom-management technique. Many trauma survivors, especially those with CPTSD, get overwhelmed if they are being treated with techniques based on psychodrama or emotional expression, or with techniques that are too rapid. Approach and timing are everything in treatment, especially when dealing with trauma disorders.

Biological Methods

While there is no single pill to take for a trauma disorder, there are many helpful biological and medical tools. Before we had much knowledge concerning trauma disorders, benzodiazepines were frequently prescribed. Benzodiazepines are addictive and are no longer recommended for almost the entire continuum of trauma disorders. Although they temporarily provide freedom from anxiety, the risk of becoming addicted to them is far too great. Therefore, in all but the most unusual circumstances, benzodiazepines should be avoided in treating trauma disorders, especially if there is a risk for an established addictive disorder.

Perhaps the most effective medications for trauma disorders are the SSRIs. These antidepressant medicines provide a boost in mood, brighten affect, and diminish obsessive thinking. Finding the right medicine and dose can take some time and effort.

Sleep disruption is a common problem with trauma disorders. Nonaddictive sleep medication can help patients get a good night's sleep and provide a tremendous boost in mood, spirit, and sense of manageability. It is vital that the medications used are not addictive. In most instances, the need for sleep medication is temporary.

If trauma survivors continue to have surges of mood swings, depression, agitation, and anxiety, the use of a mood stabilizer can be very effective. Trauma interrupts the mechanisms that help keep mood balanced and carefully managed. Mood stabilizers include Neurontin, Lamictal, and lithium.

For those individuals who have extremely severe episodes of trauma intrusion, namely extreme flashbacks coupled with unrelenting anxiety and exhaustion, short-term use of antipsychotic medications is sometimes indicated. These powerful medications can ease profound anxiety, help reestablish a sleep cycle, and give a foundation for additional healing. Used for as short a time as possible, antipsychotics do not "block" emotional processing. Instead, they permit necessary grounding for other techniques to become more effective.

Natural Methods

The same natural techniques that help anxiety, depression, ADD, and other co-occurring disorders are helpful with trauma disorders. Aerobic exercise, a balanced diet, omega-3 fatty acids, and especially breathing techniques can be powerful tools in managing trauma disorders. We strongly encourage survivors to maximize these natural techniques, which for some can replace medication. For others, these simple techniques can be an option so that medicines are not even begun. Individuals should try to use natural techniques to their maximum potential. Simple changes in lifestyle can be incredibly powerful. Careful guidance from treatment providers is necessary.

Psychological Methods

The first challenge in treating the psychological aspect of trauma disorders is determining whether the diagnosis is PTSD or CPTSD. Clinicians with expertise and experience in trauma disorders are more likely to be attuned to the differences. If your loved one has been given a diagnosis of borderline personality disorder, you are most likely dealing with CPTSD. Similarly, if a diagnosis of other personality disorders has been given, it is possible that you are really dealing with CPTSD. Seek additional evaluation if needed.

Group therapy tends to accelerate the healing process, but be careful that the group is well run and congruent with addiction recovery. Some groups err in the direction of emotional expression, which can make symptoms worse for trauma-disordered patients. Also, support groups for trauma that are not professionally facilitated can reinforce a victim mind-set. Ask the individual treatment provider whether the patient is ready for group work. Individual therapy is highly recommended as an adjunct to a group therapy process. This assists with grounding and skill building.

Treatment approaches that are helpful with simple PTSD can actually cause harm to those with CPTSD. CPTSD requires a slow, methodical approach, longer treatment, and a strong emphasis on skill building. The temperament, flexibility, patience, and style of the provider can be more important than specific techniques. Whoever provides the psychological treatment should be supportive of addiction recovery, Twelve Step work, and meetings as treatment.

Providers who use dialectical behavior therapy and cognitive-behavioral approaches tend to be well prepared to deal with PTSD and CPTSD. Exposure techniques may or may not be indicated, depending upon timing and severity of the symptoms. Methodical exposure techniques, especially when used by a trained cognitive-behavioral provider, tend to be beneficial when someone with CPTSD has gained sufficient emotional and addiction stability.

Eye Movement Desensitization and Reprocessing (EMDR) is a very popular and highly effective behaviorally based technique for treating PTSD, but it may actually make individuals with CPTSD worse if applied at the wrong time. Under the guidance of a trained therapist, EMDR pairs specific eye movements to the recollection and recitation of specific stressful memories. When an individual with CPTSD is sufficiently stable, EMDR, along with other techniques, may become applicable. As with all powerful techniques, timing and readiness are essential.

The alarms set off by the limbic system that override logic and regularly misguide trauma patients feel like gut instinct. In most instances, abrupt changes in emotional state, especially sudden surges of anger and a sudden distrust of those who were trusted, are indications that the limbic system has taken over. Patients should be instructed to trust their support system—therapists, sponsors, peer supports, select family members, and friends. Teaching symptomatic survivors to override their gut instinct will often stop a relapse to drugs or alcohol.

The overall key to successful psychological intervention with CPTSD is the building of sufficient strength in emotional containment. Part of the top-down idea we mentioned with anxiety disorders—skill building and empowering the higher levels of brain function—helps to regulate the emotional surges that are big problems for trauma survivors. The balance of expression and containment is the hallmark of effective treatment.

Interpersonal Methods

Symptomatic survivors isolate emotionally, but establishing and deepening personal supports is part of the healing process. The most symptomatic individuals will require individual therapy to start, but some may be ready for group therapy. The group process tends to speed up trauma treatment. Participation in Twelve Step meetings can be helpful for both the addictive disorder and the trauma disorder. However, trauma survivors may be more selective about which meetings they attend and whom they choose as sponsors. In some communities, AA and NA have specific groups composed mostly of sexual abuse and trauma survivors; some of these groups are gender specific. These recovery groups are not substitutes for formal therapy, group or individual, but they can help. Joining a group of recovering addicts who have been through traumatic circumstances has a normalizing effect.

Individual therapy, although oriented toward symptom management, should also be oriented toward changing the tendency to isolate. Increased comfort with disclosure and accepting help from the therapist can extend beyond the individual session. In fact, good providers actively encourage the deepening of outside supports and the building of natural support systems. It's important to keep trauma patients focused on finding healthy supports. Many individuals who suffer from CPTSD and addiction tend to seek out a hero who will fix them. In most instances, they choose the least likely candidate.

Blurring the Lines

As with all co-occurring disorders, the combination of trauma and addiction results in a blend of symptoms and overlapping dynamics. Genetic factors, age, the intensity of the trauma, and the duration of exposure determine how powerful a role the stress or addiction will play. Trauma can contribute to, not cause, the onset of the addictive disorder. Similarly, addiction can set off the circumstances that will result in trauma symptoms for some individuals. Exactly how these two conditions interact is still unclear, but it is clear they travel together and can intensify each other.

As with other co-occurring disorders, the types of chemicals used can increase the likelihood of residual damage. For example, the use of stimulants and hallucinogens can increase the odds of brain injury associated with anxiety, depression, and, as mentioned in chapter 1, hallucinogen persisting perception disorder (HPPD). Active trauma symptoms can trigger an addiction relapse in early recovery. The physical injury associated with drugs, in addition to exposure to dangerous circumstances, will contribute additional damage to the systems involved in brain regulation.

Individuals who develop PTSD and especially those who develop the more serious form, CPTSD, tend to have depression, symptoms of anxiety, distortions of perception, and sometimes even lapses in the perception of reality. It is not uncommon for individuals with CPTSD to have as many as four or five other diagnoses in addition to addiction.

Summary

PTSD is an anxiety-based syndrome that includes symptoms of a varying range and intensity. Defined simply as "a normal set of reactions to abnormal events," the emphasis is upon the event rather than the defect of the individual. The more severe variant, CPTSD, is more often observed as co-occurring with addiction. Approximately 25 to 33 percent of addicts have or have had trauma-related symptoms.

PTSD sometimes involves a delay of onset; this time delay sometimes confuses survivors and observers. Although many treatments work very well, the condition tends to come and go, especially with exposure to triggers, which can include anniversaries of the traumatic event. Many symptoms seem illogical because they involve avoidance *and* seeking of challenge, sometimes alternating with considerable speed. CPTSD has deeper impact in all areas of functioning and tends to be highly disruptive to interpersonal relationships and spiritual systems.

Trauma disorders can be the result of an addictive disorder. An addiction may be more likely to result, or develop more rapidly, as the result of symptom-producing trauma. Although the exact mechanisms are not clear, these conditions affect one another.

Exposure to a traumatic circumstance can result in the onset of trauma disorders in some individuals. Overall, 25 percent of those who experience profound overload will develop lasting symptoms. How likely this is to occur depends upon the intensity, duration, frequency, and age of exposure as well as some other variables, including genetic sensitivity and strength of support systems. Certain types of events, especially those that are man-made, greatly increase the likelihood of symptoms. The younger a person is when the event takes place, the greater the likelihood the trauma will have a potent impact. Those who develop addictions are at risk for additional trauma exposure. Individuals with addiction and trauma disorders are more likely to have CPTSD. CPTSD is identical to borderline personality disorder, which is discussed in chapter 8. CPTSD may also be connected to other personality diagnoses, including antisocial personality disorder.

Recommendations

Addiction treatment is the first step needed to deal with this co-occurring combination. Treatment for trauma should begin as soon as possible after that; untreated trauma disorders tend to result in relapse if the trauma disorder is not treated within six months of addiction treatment. Accurate diagnosis is critical in determining the correct course of trauma treatment. Treatments that help PTSD may make CPTSD worse, increasing the risk for relapse. Skill building rather than emotional expression is most effective with trauma disorders. There are many effective treatments for trauma disorders. Treatment should incorporate multiple strategies including biological (natural when possible), psychological, group support, and spiritual dialogue. Much of this can be integrated and is already built into the Twelve Steps, but some specialized treatments and supports are often necessary.

Additional treatments may be needed for the multiple combinations of other conditions that tend to go along with CPTSD and addiction, including ADHD, anxiety disorders, mood disorders (especially the atypical variant), sleep disorders, obsessive-compulsive disorders, eating disorders, body distortions (known as body dysmorphia), somatic illness (including fibromyalgia and some autoimmune disorders), sleep disorders, and depression. Some trauma survivors even hear voices but are not psychotic. Families need to be prepared to deal with a wide range of overlapping symptoms, diagnoses, and co-occurring disorders.

Look for providers who understand both disorders, and if none are available, find specialists who can work together. Trauma disorders and addiction require a sustained team approach to achieve good outcomes. Successful treatment of PTSD and CPTSD can be a key contribution in improving long-term sobriety. It is also our opinion that trauma disorders may be the linchpin with many of the other co-occurring conditions. Simply stated, we need to recognize and attend to a trauma-related disorder as a powerful and frequent co-occurring condition. With accurate diagnosis, quality treatment, and a focus on integrated approaches, we may be able to help addicts who previously resisted recovery. In addition, we may be able to interrupt the progression of both disorders. We have seen some amazing recoveries, and we are optimistic that increased attention, awareness, and prompt treatment will make a huge contribution.

Case History

Roger was back in the drunk tank once again. It was a yearly ritual. He would drink to a near-blackout level and then drive in an area he knew was well patrolled. Roger had completed primary treatment six years earlier. He was a model citizen, responsible, active in his community, and active in AA. His probation officer was frustrated—how could such a nice guy keep doing the exact same thing once a year, every year? Did he *want* to get caught? In exasperation, the probation officer insisted that Roger get some psychological help. The fact that Roger had served in Vietnam made the probation officer suspicious. Roger entered our treatment program, annoyed but cooperative. The clinical interview was difficult; Roger had a great deal of fear. Roger resented any suggestion that his drinking was connected in any way to his experiences in Vietnam. For him this was history, not to be discussed. About an hour into a very delicate interview, Roger was able to talk about something that had been hidden for decades. In early 1969, Roger had been assigned to guard his unit's perimeter. It was just after the Tet Offensive, and there had been reports of children carrying explosives in backpacks. Roger saw a young girl, about nine years of age and carrying a backpack, running toward their position. She was alone, and the backpack looked suspicious. Roger told her to stop, but she kept running toward him and his unit. He fired a single shot, killing her instantly. The girl did have powerful explosives in her pack. Roger had done what he needed to do to save his unit, and his commanders praised him. He did not think about it again, at least not until his own daughter turned six—when she was about the same size as the nine-year-old Vietnamese girl.

As Roger told me (Jeff Jay) this story, he cried and could not be consoled. He did not want to blame his drinking on this event, but I gently let him know there was a connection. He was going through an anniversary reaction, something all survivors do. I worked with Roger individually for a few weeks, and then he joined a trauma group. Although it was not easy, Roger began to feel slightly better, and eventually much better. Connecting the dots was only the beginning, but it was a powerful beginning. Each anniversary, Roger struggles but does not engage in self-destructive drinking. He remains sober, and he takes great pride in sponsoring others with combat and other trauma issues. The nightmares are gone, but some pain is never fully resolved.

10

Attention Deficit Disorder (ADD) and Addiction

As a five- or six-year-old child, I needed to be entertained 'cause I was Ritalin Boy. They didn't call it ADD when I was growing up . . . that's how I spelled DAD.

Mark Lundholm, comedian
From "Addicted Pieces" 2005

Comedian Mark Lundholm gives us an entertaining look at how ADD works in concert with addiction. He talks openly about the funny and sad circumstances he faced growing up in an alcoholic family. Constantly told to focus, he could not function in the same way others did. His arduous journey to recovery and his mastery of rapid-fire thinking have resulted in a highly successful career. One of his many creative routines focuses on FTW, which stands for "first thought wrong," his description of a core problem for addicts with ADD. These first thoughts can lead to inappropriate comments and embarrassing disclosures.

ADD (which we are using synonymously with ADHD, the variant with hyperactive motor behavior) is a neurological disorder that is present from childhood and includes impulsivity, problems with concentration, forgetfulness, and considerable cognitive inconsistency. Other core ADD symptoms include chronic underachievement, inconsistent performance, poor focus followed by hyperfocus, a tendency toward sensation seeking, a lack of patience, difficulty learning from mistakes, distractibility, day-dreaming, restlessness, unusual sleep patterns, and difficulty staying organized and on task. People with ADD tend to be late, disorganized, and sometimes absentminded. Although problems with attention and focus happen to everyone occasionally, individuals with ADD struggle with most of these symptoms at a higher intensity and with much greater consistency.

Those who have ADD also tend to be very creative and can size up complex questions with great speed. The rapid cognitive style can permit extreme focus and selective but concentrated attention. Some highly accomplished entrepreneurs and artists have full-blown ADD.

It's possible that the problem is not a deficit of attention but a surplus of attention. The extreme rate of processing and the jumping from one area of focus to another result in a string of partially completed thoughts and projects. Individuals with ADD are easily bored and crave stimulation. Many are highly creative and intelligent but have difficulty performing in school settings and conventional jobs.

ADD is a real, genetically influenced disorder that is relatively new to clinicians' vocabulary. A generation ago, this condition was called minimal brain dysfunction, a condemning and discouraging label. Widely misunderstood, misdiagnosed, and over- and underdiagnosed, ADD affects millions of individuals.

Following are some quick facts:

+ ADD is an unequivocally real phenomenon that afflicts up to 8 percent of the U.S. population.
+ About 75 percent of cases are attributed to genetics.
+ A great number of people have ADD characteristics but fall short of the official diagnosis.
+ Treatment for ADD does not necessarily include medication.
+ ADD improves in response to environmental management and improved self-care.

+ Medications work for about 80 percent of those diagnosed with ADD.
+ Certain medications may be contraindicated if an addiction has been identified, but there are safe, nonaddicting medication options.
+ Sixty percent of children diagnosed with ADD continue to have symptoms into adulthood.
+ Untreated or undiagnosed ADD can devastate self-esteem.
+ ADD does not mean dyslexia, although many individuals suffer from both disorders.
+ ADD and bipolar disorder look very similar, but mistaking one for the other could result in the wrong treatment.
+ Males are diagnosed with ADD three times more often than females.
+ Drugs and alcohol can damage the brain and worsen symptoms of ADD.
+ For those who have ADD, estimates are that
  25 percent also have a mood disorder
  40 percent are also alcoholics; 20 percent are addicted to other drugs
  50 percent are nicotine dependent
  20 percent have dyslexia
  15 percent have been also diagnosed with antisocial personality disorder (APD)
+ The majority of those with ADD may also have some form of post-traumatic stress disorder (PTSD).
+ Some studies suggest a link between ADD, learning disabilities, and fetal alcohol syndrome.

Biological Factors

ADD is clearly a neurologically based and biologically driven condition. People with ADD process information very differently than the average person. They process information with great speed but have difficulty maintaining a consistent focus, unless the stimuli involved qualify for their heightened focus. There is a definite genetic aspect; the condition runs in family lines. The more direct relatives with the condition, the more likely children are to develop it.

Recent research reveals that the brains of people with ADD are aroused in different areas. Brain images called positron emission tomography (PET) scans show definite differences in specific brain sites associated with information processing and balance. Specifically, those with ADD exhibit differences in the frontal lobes and the corpus callosum. The frontal lobes are involved with information processing, and the corpus callosum deals with left-right brain cross talk. Although the data is not yet strong enough for diagnostic purposes, these results fit perfectly with the differences in brain anatomy we'd expect to find based on the sorts of functional difficulties encountered by those with ADD.

Several developing technologies will eventually allow diagnosticians to actually see ADD at work in the brain. A quantitative electroencephalogram (QEEG) creates an electrical mapping of the brain. Used alone, the tool is not sufficient to confirm an ADD diagnosis, but it can be helpful in situations of diagnostic uncertainty. Single photon emission computed tomography (SPECT) scans appear to have some potential for diagnosis, although the results are early. Currently, these scans are available only at select clinics and some university-based facilities, but before long, brain imaging is likely to be a standard part of all ADD evaluations.

Environmental Factors

ADD may be set in motion by a head injury, lead exposure, or fetal alcohol syndrome (excessive alcohol consumption by one's mother during pregnancy). It is also believed that certain allergies, chemical toxins, and excessive exposure to television or video games make the condition worse.

Individuals with ADD who use chemicals to self-medicate get short-term relief with a large consequence. Specific chemicals, especially those that are known to damage the neocortex, seem to make ADD symptoms worse. Those who use inhalants, hallucinogens, crack cocaine, or methamphetamine seem to have worse ADD symptoms, and the damage left by the chemicals probably adds to symptom severity. Alcohol, although often slower acting, also will damage key areas of the brain involved in attention and information processing. The science is not yet precise enough to tell us how much damage is done to an individual, but we have little doubt that the addiction process will worsen ADD symptoms.

Psychological Factors

ADD is not caused by psychological issues such as sibling rivalry or conflicts with one's mother, but certain conditions, such as an anxiety disorder, depression, or post-traumatic stress disorder, can make ADD more pronounced and harder to treat. ADD is a condition that involves disjointed, sometimes frenetic, but rational thinking, not a problem with mood. This is one way sharp diagnosticians can distinguish ADD from bipolar disorder, a particularly important distinction with children. The dividing line between thinking and feeling is not always precise, and with adults we observe some overlap between the conditions, sometimes made worse by the brain damage caused by drug use.

Information processing and focus is something most people take for granted. Those who have ADD have multiple thoughts and competing impulses, images, and sensory input. This permits an often unique and creative way of looking at things, but it also results in poor organization skills and difficulty in academic settings. Those who have ADD often have very poor self-esteem. They see themselves as disorganized, deficient, and out of sync with everyone else. Although poor self-esteem is not a cause, it certainly contributes to the desire to escape with self-medication, thereby contributing to the onset of addiction. Those who have

ADD have a head start in shame-based thinking, something we commonly observe with the disease of addiction.

Interpersonal Factors

Those who have ADD tend to have a harder time making close, lasting attachments. Partners can see them as high-maintenance individuals who are not attuned to their partners' needs or way of thinking. In addition, the shame-based assumptions that most sufferers from ADD live with create a tendency to isolate and avoid connections in the first place.

Spiritual Factors

Not surprisingly, those who have ADD and an addictive disorder are disconnected, often depressed, negative, and cynical. Many suffer from nihilism, a profound emptiness. The spiritual vacuum so often seen with addiction is intensified with those who felt shame and hopelessness before they began using chemicals.

ADD and Addiction: How Are They Connected?

I have already cautioned that addictions are common in adults who have ADD, and that near-addictions and intermittent substance abuse are more the rule than the exception. This may be because of an inborn physiological problem that makes finding pleasure in ordinary ways much more difficult for the person who has ADD than for the person who doesn't have it.
Edward M. Hallowell, M.D., and John J. Ratey, M.D.
From *Driven to Distraction*

Edward Hallowell and John Ratey, authors of *Driven to Distraction*, talk about the "itch" at the core of ADD—"the itch that cannot be scratched." This itch is described as the need to put impulses into action and to change one's mood. People with ADD will do anything to quickly change an unpleasant inner feeling or a feeling of boredom. When people with ADD feel a need to escape from their feelings—to scratch the itch—they will blurt out inappropriate comments, pick an argument, or drink large quantities of alcohol. Their compulsion is beyond rational control; they put themselves at risk in order to deal with this internal crisis.

The itch idea is based on a theory called reward deficiency syndrome (RDS). RDS is a novel way of describing a wide range of impulse-driven behaviors, urges, and their consequences. It is a theory grounded in genetics and chemistry. According to the theory, people with RDS do not feel pleasure from mild to moderate levels of stimulation because of an inherited problem with dopamine, a brain chemical that allows us to feel pleasure. To feel stimulated, they take more risks and often resort to drugs. A dopamine deficiency is believed by some experts to be one of the core underpinnings of ADD.

While the RDS theory makes a great deal of sense on the surface, it is far from accepted or proven. It is likely, however, that RDS is associated with ADD and may be a core part of alcoholism, gambling addiction, sensation seeking, sociopathy, Tourette's syndrome, autism, antisocial personality disorder, schizoid personality disorder, and post-traumatic stress disorder, among others. The impulsiveness, or the itch that cannot be scratched, does appear to be a common thread in many disorders.

What is really interesting is that Hallowell and Ratey talk about "near-addict" levels of ADD. For these ADD sufferers who may have used chemicals and displayed compulsive behaviors, but are not full-blown addicts, they talk about a "new use" for the Twelve Steps. These nonaddict ADD sufferers, according to the authors' recommendations, can benefit from the core solutions of the Twelve Steps. Hallowell and Ratey brilliantly modify the steps for ADD-afflicted non- or near-addicts.

At our facility, where we deal with complex individuals who have had multiple relapses, we estimate 80 percent or more of our patients have ADD features, and most would qualify for an ADD diagnosis, along with a few other conditions. ADD is definitely a common feature in addiction.

The certainty of a scientific link between ADD and addiction gives us a huge advantage: We can assert with great confidence that neither ADD nor addiction is caused by a lack of motivation or willpower. In fact, the accusations of laziness or lack of character only add to the shame and reinforce the problem.

Treating ADD

As with all co-occurring disorders, multidisciplinary and multi-provider approaches are more likely to succeed.

Biological Methods

A clinician's first thought when treating ADD is usually to prescribe medication. ADD has received a lot of press, with articles saying that it is overdiagnosed and that the medications are addictive and may have serious, long-term side effects. The bottom line is this:

1. Medication does help to temper ADD symptoms, especially in children.
2. ADD is sometimes diagnosed in kids who are simply unruly.
3. For people who don't need medication but are given it anyway, there's a risk of fueling addiction. We have no evidence to support this, but it is logical and reflects the concerns and reports of many parents.
4. Solid evidence shows that proper medication for those who really have ADD actually *prevents* the onset of addiction. This is also logical. If children can be spared the internal chaos and self-esteem-shattering consequences of ADD, they are less likely to seek self-medication or to be seduced by addictive behaviors and peers.

Medications that stimulate the brain actually help those with ADD to focus. The most commonly used medicines for ADD are direct stimulants such as Adderall, Ritalin, and Concerta. These are safe and effective for most, but they are contraindicated if there is a diagnosed addictive disorder because these medications are too easily manipulated, snorted, and abused. The longer-acting variants that release medication slowly may be less readily abused, but they are still too dangerous to be given to addicts.

Addicts can use nonstimulant ADD medications, which include Wellbutrin and Strattera, safely and effectively. Effexor and Cymbalta are effective for those who have ADD, addiction, and features of mixed depression. For some individuals, the SSRIs provide symptom relief from ADD. SSRIs are particularly helpful if depression co-occurs with ADD. Prozac, an activating SSRI, appears to be especially effective. However, many individuals need to add another medicine, a stimulant or mood stabilizer, to maintain therapeutic progress. For addicts, nonaddictive stimulants are indicated.

Medication helps approximately 80 percent of people diagnosed with ADD, a figure not too far off from the estimates of depressed people who respond to antidepressants. Medication alone, however, does not usually do the job. In addition to medicine, a careful diet—one which includes omega-3 supplements and avoids excessive carbohydrates—and aerobic exercise are highly recommended. Aerobic exercise appears to be a necessity, not an option, for those who have ADD and addiction. Specific balance-related exercises can reportedly stimulate the cerebellum and help with attention. These exercises include yoga and tai chi. For the 20 percent of the ADD population who do not respond to or choose not to take medication, these natural biological options are vital.

Psychological Methods

Psychotherapy can be a major contribution in helping to heal the consequences of ADD and addiction. Sessions would most likely

deal with broken relationships and shattered self-esteem and provide support and direction for lifestyle changes. The goals of formal therapy should include rebuilding the devastated ego (sense
of inferiority) that so many have, often because of a failure to fin-
ish projects or to get a diploma.

As with most co-occurring conditions, we recommend a more
practical, cognitive-behavioral approach along with accurate feedback, ongoing diagnostic input, support, validation, education,
and acceptance. No single style of psychotherapy is necessarily superior, but it should be noted that most addicts, especially those
with ADD, do not respond well to long silences and ambiguous
responses. Classically trained analytic providers, or those with an
existential (Rogerian) background, often focus on reflecting feelings and encouraging the patient to articulate feelings. This style
tends to irritate individuals with ADD. A more interactive, playful, reciprocal dialogue with clear feedback works best.

In some instances, an organizational coach can be a helpful addition to a formal therapy process. People with ADD need a push
to get organized and to be efficient and accountable. Sometimes
this involves the assistance of loved ones or family members; often
it involves the services of a coach or organization facilitator. The
goal is progress, not perfection, and this should be clearly stated
as part of the clinical contract. Addicts and those with ADD tend
to have a black-and-white perspective; they want things fixed,
right now, and perfectly. If that doesn't happen, they tend to give
up and disconnect, seek chaos, or use. Disentangling this internal
conditioning and internal dialogue is an important part of relapse
prevention.

Interpersonal Methods

The fellowship of AA can be an incredibly powerful tool in
helping with ADD and addiction, as the following quote from
Delivered from Distraction, by Edward M. Hallowell and John J.
Ratey, illustrates.

I will never forget what one man said to me, a man who had both ADD and an addiction to narcotics. After he joined a 12-step program he was able to give up his addiction. He has been clean and sober for more than twenty years. He explained to me that abstinence was one part of the program. "Most people think of the 12 steps in terms of what you give up. But the truth is, you get back much more than you give up."

"Okay," I argued, "but you still did have to give up something you used to like an awful lot, something that had given you bursts of pleasure, even though it was also killing you. How did you give up the drugs? What did you turn to instead for the high they used to give you?"

"Fellowship," he replied instantly. He didn't have to think for even a fraction of a second. This was not a man who would parrot what he'd been taught. He had truly discovered a better high in fellowship than he had found in drugs.

Those fortunate enough to accept the fellowship of AA will derive the benefits of group support, encouragement, and validation. Because so many addicts have partial or full-blown ADD, many uplifting and validating stories are likely to be disclosed during meetings. Addressing and sometimes confronting the loneliness or uniqueness that suffering folks experience is a potent healing agent. This general principle, called universality, helps those who suffer in quiet desperation and with feelings of uniqueness to know they are not alone. The fellowship of AA is healing in that others mirror the same struggle. Many of the stories told at meetings are funny, painful, poignant, and consistent with the human condition, especially when chaos—internal, external, or due to ADD—is part of the picture. Feeling connected and no longer unique can heal injury, reinforce change, and encourage forward movement and sustained sobriety. The fellowship of AA is more than an exchange of war stories. It is a process of connection and validation that helps people to feel normal.

Spiritual Methods

As with all co-occurring or singular disorders, a healthy spirituality, whatever it's based on, can help quiet the internal noise. Feeling as if things can get better, believing that there are forces beyond our control or perception, and awaiting inspiration rather than pursuing danger help almost all co-occurring combinations. The flexibility of AA is particularly helpful for those with ADD. It permits creative, sometimes rebellious, and highly original individuals to derive a vision and description of their own Higher Power. People with ADD may intuitively resist structured and rule-driven religions. It may be that the spirituality of AA is a product of an ADD cognitive style. The only rule is to stay sober.

Blurring the Lines

ADD and addiction are connected. As with all forms of co-occurring disorders, it is difficult to discern which condition drives which. ADD can be the result of using certain chemicals, or it can be a contributing force for the onset of an addictive disorder. ADD is associated with numerous conditions, including addiction, depression, anxiety disorder, and post-traumatic stress disorder. So how are all of these conditions interconnected? Are they genetic, or does environment play an important role? The answer, as we have seen with so many forms of double trouble, is: We do not know. The reward deficiency syndrome is an interesting idea but only describes a characteristic that is part of all co-occurring disorders.

We do know that the journey into addiction complicates an ADD diagnosis even more. For example, someone with ADD who becomes addicted might develop a mood disorder as a result of damage from the use of drugs. If a provider then prescribes a stimulant, things might improve temporarily, with glowing reports of improved focus. The stimulant, however, might then set off a mania, a depression, or a relapse of addiction. Navigating the realm of uncertainty is the core of surviving co-occurring disorders, especially when ADD combines with its partners.

Summary

ADD is a well-established, biologically driven phenomenon that can interrupt efficiency and clarity for those who have it. Although we all have episodes of ADD, and many addicts have features of ADD, the full-blown disorder can be devastating in terms of self-esteem and can result in underperformance in many areas of life, especially in school settings. ADD is associated with impulsivity, daydreaming, procrastination, and disorganization, or what some would call "sloth." We now know that this cognitive style can facilitate creativity and seems to help some entrepreneurs see the big picture right away.

Those who have ADD are at very high risk for developing addictive disorders, or near-addictive disorders. Although there are many addicts with full-blown ADD, it may be that there are even more who suffer from near-ADD. What unifies these disorders is not yet clear. It is interesting that both groups have a higher incidence of PTSD. We also know that there is a correlation of mood disorders in all of these groups, and that accurate differential diagnosis is very important. ADD coupled with addiction causes disruption in thinking, biology, and support and spiritual systems.

Many believe that stimulant medication is the only form of treatment for ADD. While stimulants usually work very well for nonaddicts, they are not the only medicine, and medicines are not the sole foundation for successful treatment. Those who have ADD or ADD with addiction need more than just medication; a good treatment plan encompasses multiple strategies and providers.

Recommendations

ADD is highly treatable, but the treatments that work for nonaddicts should not be given to addicts. Stimulant medication can result in temporary relief, but it often sets off a cascade of addictive behaviors and relapse. Although the time-released stimulants are better, they are still not safe to use with the vast majority of addicts. Nonstimulant options are highly effective.

Medication for ADD only or for ADD with a co-occurring condition must be blended with a highly structured treatment plan. There are numerous nonmedicinal therapies that affect biology. These include attention to exercise and diet. Those who have this form of co-occurring disorder need directed physical activity, not only talk or written work.

We highly recommend psychotherapy with an engaging, communicative provider who will help identify necessary changes in behavior and interpersonal style. Rebuilding self-esteem, goal setting, and finding engaging, stimulating, meaningful, and playful outlets are a vital part of recovery.

Structure is an exceptionally important consideration. While nobody does well with boredom, those with ADD, especially addicts with ADD, do not do well without structure. Most good addiction treatment programs have a tight, comprehensive, and—for average folks—rather exhausting schedule. Having too much time, and specifically too much time to think, simply adds to confusion. Multiple streams of thought that have no focus or direction are likely to generate chaos, impulsivity, restlessness, and depression.

The comprehensive approach of AA or NA will help those who have ADD and/or addiction to feel connected and validated. AA helps to provide needed clarity and direction.

Because there is enormous overlap with ADD, addiction, depression, anxiety, and bipolar disorders, an initial diagnosis could be inaccurate. Insist upon more evaluation and testing, especially if your instincts tell you that something is wrong. Getting additional testing, including brain-imaging work—through a SPECT, PET, or QEEG—and providing the treatment team or diagnosticians with as much family history and developmental history as possible will help to ensure an accurate diagnosis. Finally, be prepared for the possibility that while participating in the diagnosis and treatment of a loved one, a family member might discover that he or she has near-ADD, near-addiction, or full-blown variants of these conditions.

Case History

At thirty-seven years of age, Manny was a very successful entrepreneur. His business was flourishing, but his life was falling apart. He had come from a solidly middle-class background and worked in his early years as an auto mechanic. Now he owned a national franchise of repair shops, an estate-sized home, and a beautiful yacht. At the same time, he was no longer able to come to work because of his alcoholism, and his wife was very close to filing for divorce. His teenage children called him "MIA," which sometimes meant "missing in action," "Manny in action," or just "manic." How did all this come about?

Manny suffered from undiagnosed ADD. As an adolescent, he did poorly in school but excelled in the things that interested him. Early on, cars were his hobby, and he quickly became an expert in all things related to automotive performance. This naturally led to mechanical work, and when he dropped out of high school, he got a job at a local garage.

Manny was also prone to great ideas and bursts of energy. It seemed there was nothing he couldn't do if he really wanted to do it. His enthusiasm was contagious, and it wasn't long before he talked his grandfather into loaning him the money necessary to open his own shop. Manny was good at business and found that he enjoyed making money more than working on cars. Before long, he was devoting all his energy to opening one repair shop and then another. He was lucky to find a good secretary early on, because he was unable to organize details or pay attention to tedious items such as taxes and payroll. If the truth be told, the secretary ran the business while Manny supplied the energy necessary to find the next round of financing.

Manny had charmed his high school sweetheart into marriage by the age of twenty. They began having children right away, and he started losing interest in the relationship, concentrating instead on his business. He also made a new friend, alcohol, which helped him unwind at the end of the day. It seemed perfect to Manny. He worked like a demon, provided an idyllic lifestyle for his family, and drank good scotch at night.

He'd never been a big drinker in the earliest years of the business, and he often worked twelve hours a day. With a new business and a new family, neither Manny nor his wife realized how sleep disturbed he really was; he often got by on four or five hours of sleep per night. When he finally discovered alcohol, it seemed like an answer to a prayer. He wasn't a live wire at midnight anymore, but instead he was able to start winding down right after dinner. The alcohol made everything seem better, and so he kept drinking. Within a few years, Manny became dependent on alcohol. No one noticed outside his household, and he was still a powerhouse in business. His wife complained, but he said she was unsympathetic about his work and ungrateful for all he provided.

Several years passed before his drinking started interfering with business. By that time, his wife was ready to leave him. He drank seven days a week, his marital relationship was basically nonexistent, and he was rarely at the office. Manny bought a large yacht after he opened his twenty-fifth repair shop, and he often drank alone on the boat, complaining that no one understood him.

Manny's secretary and two of his closest friends finally organized an intervention. Family members participated too, making for a well-rounded intervention team. His wife was convinced that Manny was bipolar and insisted on a dual diagnosis facility. But when he was fully evaluated by the psychologist and the rest of the multidisciplinary team, it became evident that Manny wasn't bipolar, but was suffering from attention deficit disorder in addition to alcoholism.

During his treatment, Manny was prescribed an anti-depressant, an SSRI, which helped to stabilize his thinking. It also helped him find the patience to participate meaningfully in group therapy. Manny was quick to find differences with other patients and tried to compare himself out from the rest of the group. But by the time he finished his third week in treatment, he began to make friends and realized that he really wasn't so different from everyone else.

After treatment, continued involvement in AA was the key to Manny's success. He found an early-morning meeting that was frequented by businesspeople Monday through Friday. This was the perfect way for him to start the day, and it also left him free in the evening to spend time with his wife and children.

With his continuing sobriety, Manny's medication was cut down to a very low dose. Gradually, he developed an interest in improving his diet and exercise regimen as well. Now, Manny and his family look forward to spending time on the boat, snorkeling, and windsurfing in the summertime. Manny keeps up with his teenage boys now, and the epithet "MIA" hasn't been heard in a very long time.

11

Head Trauma and Brain Injury

During my drinking days, I can't tell you how many fights I was in. I was knocked out a few times, but I couldn't tell you if it was just a blackout. I crashed my car five times, fell down the stairs, and split my skull on the edge of a coffee table. I had a CT scan after the second car crash, but that was about it. My concentration is pretty bad now, and I can't stay organized the way I used to when I still had my law practice.

Nathan, age 42, recovering alcoholic

Test your knowledge of co-occurring disorders by answering the following question: In a person with a co-occurring disorder, significant changes in attitude, behavior, concentration, job performance, and emotional stability are due to

a. the progression of the disease of addiction

b. brain damage due to the use of alcohol, inhalants, hallucinogens, or other drugs

c. a mental illness set off by addiction, trauma, or brain injury

d. a brain injury due to an accident while sober or intoxicated

e. a brain injury due to a medical condition, such as a blood clot, hemorrhaging, tumor, or disease

f. all of the above

"F" is the right answer, but in our experience, "d," a brain injury due to an accident, is often minimized, forgotten, or overlooked.

Many addicts and alcoholics—either because of denial, shame, or blackouts—ignore falls and accidents that eventually result in cumulative brain injury. Some individuals begin drinking and drugging after an accident, often car or motorcycle, because of brain injury and/or emotional aftermath. Many head injuries do not reach the doctor or emergency room and escape formal evaluation. Without an observed loss of consciousness, a head injury episode might be missed or dismissed by patients, families, or health care providers as inconsequential. In some instances, significant damage occurs and does not receive the level of testing needed. Undetected head injuries can result in behaviors that are confusing to the outside observer and may be mistaken as manipulation or medication seeking. It's not unusual for casualties of head trauma to wind up addicted and homeless, especially if the head trauma goes undetected.

A young man who crashed his motorcycle while intoxicated did not have visible scars from his accident, but he was no longer functioning well enough to hold a job. He was dropped from Social Security Disability Insurance, and his family members no longer supported him because of his continued drinking. They were simply following a course of tough love. With no money and no ability to obtain or hold a job, he joined the ranks of the homeless. A substantial number of homeless, nonpsychotic substance-abusing individuals have subtle neurological deficits.

What Is Head Trauma?

Head trauma happens when a direct blunt force comes into contact with the head. The brain is protected by several layers, composed of tissue, bone, and fluid, but a traumatic impact to the head, whether it produces open wounds or not, can damage the brain. Head injuries may be open or closed, and both can be life-threatening. An open injury may expose the various layers that protect the brain. Visible head wounds usually involve a lot of bleeding because the head is very vascular. Skull fractures may not be visible but usually produce visible signs, such as dark bruises around the eyes or behind an ear. A closed injury may involve internal bleeding, leakage of cerebrospinal fluid, a contusion (bruise) of the brain, or a fractured skull. A hematoma is a collection of blood or fluid that is the result of injury or a spontaneous rupture of a blood vessel. Intracranial hematomas are accumulations of blood within the brain. An intracerebral hematoma forms deep in the brain and is common with severe head injury or stroke.

Signs and symptoms of head trauma include vomiting, combativeness, dilated or unequal pupils, blood or white fluid leaking from the ears or nose, bruises under the eyes or behind the ears, tingling or numbness in the extremities, confusion, or altered responsiveness. Loss of consciousness may or may not occur. While most minor bumps heal themselves in a few days, more severe head injuries may take between six months and a year to reach maximum improvement. Profound head injuries can result in loss of mobility, loss of speech, and sometimes clear changes in personality and cognitive functioning.

Addiction, Brain Injury, and Head Trauma

Brain injury because of head trauma may be a secondary consequence of addiction. Persisting brain injury may be a contributing factor to a change in personality, which may lead to an addiction and/or a psychiatric condition.

Evidence of repeated injury is more common among alcoholics and the elderly. Alcoholics and addicts are more likely to incur physical trauma that includes brain injury, but they may ignore seemingly mild to moderately severe injuries. This may be a function of denial or a consequence of blacking out, and it may be why we see cumulative head trauma, brain injury associated with trauma that goes undiagnosed and untreated. The risk for physical injury, especially head injury, is greatly increased as a result of intoxication.

Accidents involving the head that do not outwardly damage the skull, and may or may not involve a loss of consciousness, can still produce serious damage. The brain can be bruised or internal bleeding can create pressure within the brain, causing permanent damage. Closed-head injuries can have subtle, long-term consequences. It is the subtle damage that is often overlooked and can fuel an ongoing addiction and contribute to personality and cognitive changes that are not so obvious, at least at first. Such changes may be marked by impulsivity and moodiness. Some individuals will become more aggressive, others more withdrawn. Sometimes a head injury will create or exacerbate pain. Countless mysterious cases of relapse and co-occurring disorders are eventually associated with a history of head trauma.

Head injuries may affect very specific areas of brain function. Depending on what area of the brain is impacted, injury can be as specific as a decline in the ability to process visual information that involves dimension and perspective. Sometimes only visual memory or auditory information processing is affected.

Other causes of damage to the brain can involve central nervous system compromise. Stroke victims and people who experience transient ischemic attacks (TIAs), sometimes called ministrokes, can have peculiar effects such as garbled speech, sudden blindness in one or both eyes, double vision, weakness, paralysis, or loss of balance.

Seizure disorders can also be the consequence of head injury and have been connected to mood disorders. There is even a form of seizure disorder that is subclinical—meaning it can't be detected by normal clinical tests—that affects information processing, awareness, and consciousness for very brief periods but with no outward signs, such as the motor paralysis and convulsing so often associated with a major motor seizure.

Injury to the temporal lobes has been studied extensively. The temporal lobes are associated with many cognitive processes such as recent memory, music, language, mature decision making, higher-order judgment, and managing of emotional situations. Injury to the temporal lobe may result in the inability to handle emotion, and in some instances it can be associated with anger and violent outbursts. Specific tests can detect this type of damage.

Mild to moderate head injuries can often escape detection. It is important for clinicians, patients, and loved ones to consider the possible consequences of a head injury when trying to manage the complex realm of addiction and co-occurring disorders. Because of denial, shame, or blackouts, falls and other events that could cause head traumas may not have been reported to professionals or loved ones. We have heard many stories of addicts who walk away from car wrecks and get home without having any recollection of the impact.

In our experience, too little neuropsychological and neurological testing is performed on individuals with a history of addiction and possible head injury. If you suspect your loved one may have injured himself more than he is reporting, or if you are noticing changes in alertness, organization, memory, or information processing, you may wish to ask for additional neurological and/or neuropsychological testing, as well as diagnostic imaging work. If changes are detected by these additional tests, important changes in your loved one's treatment plan are likely to occur. Expectations for certain treatment assignments might be altered, a different set of Step materials might be used, or the length of time he will remain in treatment might be affected. In some instances, a different treatment setting might be required. In other instances, a specific medication might be added that facilitates cognitive efficiency.

Additional Testing

Undiagnosed or underdiagnosed brain injuries can result in behaviors that are confusing to the outside observer and that may be mistaken as manipulation, medication seeking, or weakness, as in the case of those who relapse chronically.

Following a head trauma, various levels of evaluation may be performed, depending upon the circumstance and severity of injury. A mild injury may not reach the threshold of a full-scale and expensive workup. Simply falling down a few stairs or hitting your head on the coffee table may not meet criteria for extensive testing. Although trips to the emergency room often result in CT scans, MRIs, MRAs, and neurological examination, more subtle injuries may not be evaluated, detected, or even detectable.

We know the brain can repair itself very well, but we also know that some injuries can result in slow, hard-to-detect changes. Whether these changes are due to the closed-head injury, subsequent chemical assaults, or some other disease process is difficult to judge. Complex addicts, many of whom have multiple psychiatric diagnoses, may have a higher incidence of head injury. It can be difficult to know when to insist on more extensive neurological brain imaging and a neuropsychological evaluation, hence the need for careful history taking. Standard testing upon entering drug treatment often includes a quick and simple measure of cognitive clarity. Short of formal IQ tests, tests such as the Shipley Institute of Living Scale are administered by many of the major treatment programs. Deficiency in either verbal performance or math/puzzle-solving skills can give some clue as to possible brain injury. In addition, the evaluators will look for a difference between verbal and performance skill, a classic soft indicator that some damage may have occurred. Disparity in results between types of cognitive performance, as well as an overall drop in pre-injury or preaddiction levels, may indicate a need for more testing. Changes in attention span are also noteworthy and may warrant specific neuropsychological tests. Then again, sometimes performance irregularities are the result of incomplete detox, learning anomalies, or ADD. If there is doubt, more testing may be appropriate.

Newer scanning methods such as fMRI (functional magnetic resonance imaging) and SPECT scans can detect changes in brain activity, not simply tissue damage. These methods one day may permit more accurate diagnosis of psychopathology, subtle brain injury, and changes in cognitive efficiency. Using these techniques to assist in psychiatric diagnosis or changes in cognitive ability is experimental, and expectations are ahead of the science, but the ability to see brain areas in action holds considerable potential. These scanning methods do not yet replace tests of mental skill and cognitive function, abilities measured by comprehensive neuropsychological testing. Some very sophisticated evaluation units use these tests in conjunction with older methods, and their data may eventually enhance accuracy and precision.

Additional testing is time consuming and expensive. A comprehensive neuropsychological workup can take several days, though most diagnostic examinations can be completed in less time with a focused referral question. The findings can be invaluable and make a difference in educating providers, the patient, and family members as to cognitive strengths and limitations, the overall effect of which is to facilitate recovery. If testing is consistent with brain damage, the patient may be referred to a specialized treatment program for cognitive and behavioral rehabilitation. A lapse in cognition or memory is different from a manipulation or drug-seeking behavior and requires specialized treatment, or at least a change in treatment pacing and assignment completion.

Brain Injury Due to Chemicals

Almost every co-occurring psychological condition we have covered in the preceding chapters includes chemical assault to the brain. It is not known how much a given toxin or state of inebriation will injure an individual brain. Patterns of neuropsychological impairment reflecting brain injury differ quite widely depending on the chemical toxin. We know, for example, that the greater the concentration of alcohol, the more frequent the use, and the more often blackouts occur, the more likely it is that there will be lasting damage, but the functional deficits resulting and the time it takes for recovery, or lack thereof, are different in binge drinkers compared with continuous drinkers, different in young people compared with older people, and different in men compared with women.

Dr. Boriskin was startled the first time he observed a twenty-nine-year-old alcoholic in a nursing home. The young man did not know the date, the name of the current president, or where he was born. According to his attending physicians, his favorite drink was Everclear, a 190-proof grain alcohol, which he consumed nightly until passing out. Most alcoholics do not progress this quickly, but when they do, the residual damage may be profound and permanent. Certainly the progression of this man's disease was hastened by the strength and quantity of the alcohol that he ingested.

The choice of chemicals and their combinations also play a role in brain injury. Inhalants, especially gasoline, are very toxic to the brain. Solvents in household chemicals and glue are commonly used as inhalants, with spray paint being a popular choice among the homeless population. The different ingredients in solvents have different neurotoxicities. Toluene is by far the most injurious. Xylene is less harmful, yet certain solvents that are innocuous in themselves can increase the neurotoxicity of others when combined.

There is substantial evidence indicating that at certain doses and intensities of use, all amphetamines—including the currently popular methamphetamine and the solvent ingredients of multiple household cleaners and flammable chemicals—damage nerve tissue.

Ecstasy, which is MDMA, is a powerful stimulant, like an amphetamine, with a hallucinogenic effect. Ecstasy advocates contend it is a completely safe drug. However, contrary to the pro-Ecstasy propaganda, there is compelling neurobiogical evidence that Ecstasy will damage brain neurons. It is interesting to note that when the National Institute on Drug Abuse (NIDA) released its first reports of brain damage due to Ecstasy, the researchers had mistakenly used data from monkeys that were administered methamphetamine (not Ecstasy). When this incon-sistency was noted, NIDA repeated the studies using MDMA and verified that Ecstasy does in fact damage brain cells. The ear-lier error is sometimes used out of context to deny the damag-ing effects of Ecstasy. The fact that the initial attempts to legislate MDMA out of public reach were based on incorrect results gave the false perception that the drug was really safe. Later studies showed that it actually is extremely neurotoxic, particularly to memory function, if chronically used. The damage to neural cir-cuits results in mood disruption (a lasting depression for many) and measurable memory deficits, as well as HPPD. Although relatively uncommon, some deaths have been associated with Ec-stasy because of the interruption of temperature regulation that accompanies its use during high-energy dance fests, conducted for hours, called raves.

The damaging effects of other hallucinogens are still being studied. LSD seems to produce acquired color confusion and other perceptual damage. Cocaine also injures brain tissue, but the injury is not as visible or as dramatic as other chemicals. However, cocaine's effects on psychological function can be persistently dev-astating and similar in quality to those produced by amphetamines. It appears that the damage is associated with the brain's pleasure centers (including the mesolimbic dopaminergic systems involv-ing the nucleus accumbens, or the core of the pleasure processing system). Long-term deleterious effects on brain anatomy are not yet known, although some clinicians believe there is a greater risk for neurodegenerative diseases such as Parkinson's disease.

On a SPECT or PET scan, the visible evidence of brain damage from inhalants is dramatic and from chronic methamphetamine use is clear. Cocaine-induced changes qualitatively resemble those induced by amphetamines, particularly on frontal and temporal lobes, and differences likely result from the briefer duration of effect of cocaine (minutes) compared with methamphetamine (hours to days). Brains exposed to lower doses of alcohol and other chemicals show more subtle damage. This may change with improved imaging technology. We do know that sustained use of almost all addictive chemicals interferes with brain function. Chronic marijuana users show cognitive deficits and brain damage after years of use.

Potent mixtures of mood-altering chemicals, sometimes in concert with eating disorders, accidents, or other physical trauma, can result in dramatic neurological damage. In numerous instances, vegetative comas are associated with drug overdose, toxic mixtures, or idiosyncratic reactions. The 1975 case of Karen Ann Quinlan was the first widely publicized instance of a vegetative coma; this was apparently due to the brain-toxic effects of alcohol and tranquilizers.

The consequences of long-term alcoholism are that the brain and/or the liver will give out; genetics likely determines which. Brain shrinkage occurs and memory is affected. The syndrome known as wet brain, or cerebral edema (swelling), is an alcoholism-related condition that may lead to a loss of short-term memory, disorientation, and confusion. It is a serious neurological consequence that often corrects itself after sufficient lengths of abstinence. Older brains tend to be less forgiving than younger brains. However, once a sufficient level of injury is incurred, and memory does not rebound after ninety days, more evaluation is indicated. The most serious form of brain injury due to chemicals is Korsakoff's psychosis, a permanent and severe memory loss coupled with confabulation, delusion, and personality changes. Chronic alcoholism, protracted blackouts, wet brain, and repeated falls (increasing the risk of repeated head injuries) likely exacerbate other degenerative brain diseases.

Summary and Recommendations

Addicts are more likely than nonaddicts to experience dramatic or subtle injury to the brain, and the process of addiction is itself due to persistent organic change in the brain. Car accidents, blackouts, falling, fights, and a whole array of addiction-related consequences greatly increase the probability of brain injury. Continued use of mood-altering chemicals adds insult to injury, the extent of which may be difficult to discern and detect for a given individual.

Certain substances are more likely to produce rapid neurological consequences, methamphetamines and inhalants in particular. Marijuana and alcohol will injure the brain with sufficient exposure over time. Traumatic head injuries usually result in extensive testing, evaluation, and treatment. Closed-head injuries may involve lower levels of immediate injury and more subtle consequences over the long term, especially with the ongoing use of addictive chemicals.

Primary treatment programs often use simple and quick screening tests that sometimes pick up consequences associated with head injury. Sometimes these tools do not detect certain types of injury. Additional testing is time consuming and expensive but may be invaluable. The consequences of head injury may be an important missing variable in a complex blend of co-occurring disorders. Neuropsychological testing, in addition to a standard neurological workup, and specific neurodiagnostic tests including EEG and brain imaging can provide invaluable information that can result in better outcomes and more precise treatment.

Case History

Despite having completed five treatment programs during a seven-year period, Alice, a fifty-three-year-old clinical social worker, could not stay sober. She knew the Big Book, understood addiction, and even understood how her childhood sexual abuse affected her judgment and perceptions. Alice's short-term memory was poor and getting worse with each relapse.

Alice became an alcoholic following a near-fatal beating during the course of her work. She had assisted the courts in the dangerous job of facilitating emergency involuntary commitments for the county courts. Alice interviewed individuals whom the courts, police, or county hospital believed were imminently dangerous to themselves or other people. Based on Alice's determination, an individual could be restrained against his or her will for a period of seventy-two hours. Given the danger of this role, Alice was always observed by law enforcement officers who would protect her from any harm. During one late-afternoon proceeding, the large deputies who watched through the two-way mirror became distracted. The highly paranoid and aggressive young man she was evaluating suddenly erupted into a violent frenzy, delivering numerous blows to Alice and rendering her unconscious. Rigorous rehabilitation restored movement to her paralyzed body. Alice's hard work resulted in a restoration of mobility and a return to cognitive clarity. Unfortunately, a profound depression ensued that left her unable to work. With nothing to occupy her time, Alice's alcohol consumption steadily increased.

Our treatment program was the sixth one Alice attended. Her prior records indicated she was manipulative and attention seeking, as well as medication seeking. Alice began complaining that she could not keep track of simple things. Despite Alice's considerable intellect, her lack of attention to detail and her confused look had us wondering what was going on. We decided to have her undergo a full neurological and neuropsychological evaluation and found that Alice's head injury had left her with specific memory and cognitive deficiencies. She had the equivalent of severe attention deficit disorder.

The neurologist suggested a stimulant, which is risky for most addicts and, as noted in chapter 10, is contrary to standard medical recommendation in most cases of ADD with addiction. Given her head injury and her risk for relapse, we decided to use the stimulant in addition to a very small dose of Antabuse, the medicine that makes people ill if they consume alcohol. We kept her on the anticonvulsant medicine she was already taking.

The neuropsychological testing helped us to distinguish between manipulation and loss of functioning. Our clinical feedback became more accurate; we were able to more accurately interpret when Alice's lack of follow-through was a neurological phenomenon, not part of a denial system. This validated what was actually happening, rather than adding to her shame and frustration. Alice's anger and frustration levels dropped significantly. With the stimulant, Alice's clarity improved remarkably. In addition, the treatment team worked with her and developed strategies to compensate for her specific memory weaknesses. Four years later, she is sober and well adjusted. Although she could not return to work—her physical, cognitive, and emotional limitations left her unable to function at a full-time job—she is able to do part-time volunteer work, which gives her a sense of meaning. If the head injury had not been attended to, chances are she would have been in her seventh or eighth treatment program by now.

12

Chronic Pain and Addiction

Pain is a total biopsychosocial experience. You hurt physically. You psychologically respond to pain by thinking, feeling, and acting. You think about the pain and try to figure out what is causing it and why you're hurting. You experience emotional reactions to the pain. You may get angry, frightened, or frustrated by your pain. You talk about your pain with family, friends, and coworkers who help you develop a social and cultural context for assigning meaning to your personal pain experience and taking appropriate action.

Stephen Grinstead, Ph.D.
From *Freedom from Suffering: Seven Strategies for Achieving Successful Pain Management*

Pain is the body's way of letting us know something is wrong with our physical being. Pain encourages us to do something to correct the ailment. Specialized cells signal the brain when something in the body's environment goes awry, creating the sensation of pain. When we touch a hot stove top, the pain we feel forces us to remove our hand before we even have a chance to think about it. Not only do we save ourselves from getting third-degree burns, but we also learn not to touch a hot stove top again. Most pain is temporary, and feeling pain can protect us from further injury or death.

Chronic pain occurs when normal, healthy pain signals become unrelenting and disruptive. Acute pain may be helpful in protecting our back, for example, from additional injury. If the pain continues, it may result in lack of use of body parts, weakening of muscles, and other negative consequences. The pain signals keep going, causing more distress than protection. Chronic pain afflicts up to 50 percent of Americans sometime during their lives. Experts differ on the transition time from acute to chronic pain: The range is anywhere from thirty days to six months. The time frame depends in part on the specific type of pain involved.

Chronic pain may or may not be the result of an identifiable injury, and two people with the exact same injury may have different levels of pain. Many people have bulging discs with no back pain, and many have excruciating pain without visible disc injury. Similarly, diseases such as fibromyalgia, a painful and sometimes debilitating condition involving muscle and connecting tissue, do not necessarily result from injury and may not be observable in tissue damage. Chronic headaches also do not result from observed injury or tissue damage for many sufferers. Due to this ambiguity, some individuals are told their pain is not real.

Chronic pain may be the result of tissue injury, nerve injury, chemical changes in the brain, scarring, biochemical changes at the site of injury, or unknown factors. Those who live with chronic pain often need to alter their lifestyles.

Biopsychosocial Aspects of Chronic Pain

Pain is a personal, subjective experience whose reality is beyond question for the vast majority of sufferers. By the same token, perception and emotion play a large role in the experience of pain. If we are depressed, anxious, lonely, or tired, any pain signals the body is producing are likely to be enhanced. The brain is where pain gets interpreted, and context, support systems, rest, expectation, and emotion play a role in the experience. This is not to say that emotions create pain; they do not. Attitude and emotional state, however, affect how pain is felt and managed. The biological part of pain involves the physical signaling process. The psychological aspect involves our thoughts, interpretations, feelings, and the meaning we assign to the pain. The social aspect involves the meaning others assign to pain—whether the pain is okay or a source of shame.

Disorders Associated with Chronic Pain

Pain has a long list of sensations. It can feel sharp, burning, jabbing, throbbing, achy, tingly, stinging, or dull. The specific type of injury may involve specific parts of the pain transmission highway, which affects medication strategy, treatment options, and rehabilitation strategies. All pain is a biopsychosocial phenomenon, yet not all pain is alike.

Various types of pain are associated with diseases, autoimmune processes, and injury. Affected individuals should learn more about their specific conditions, the causes, and treatments. Some common chronic painful conditions include neuropathy (lingering nerve pain), arthritis, back pain, complex regional pain syndrome (CRPS), endometriosis, headaches, orofacial pain, irritable bowel syndrome, carpal tunnel syndrome, and cystitis. The pain associated with these and other conditions can be excruciating and debilitating.

Pain Management

Pain, whether acute or chronic, and whether the result of illness, accident, or surgery, is usually initially handled in the hospital or doctor's office with a prescription for pain medication. The most common painkillers are the opiates, or opioids, also known as narcotics. If the pain becomes chronic, patients are sometimes sent to pain management programs.

Opiates as Pain Medication

Opiates, more accurately synthetic opiates, including Darvocet, Vicodin, Percocet, Lorcet, and OxyContin, are highly effective medications when properly used for the management of acute pain. Opiates are often prescribed following surgery because their ability to block pain helps patients get out of bed sooner, which contributes to healing. While necessary and appropriate for some individuals and certain conditions, opiates can cause problems when taken for chronic pain. Problems include rebound pain and hyperalgesia, a heightened perception of pain, when they are discontinued. Another potential problem is that opiates are addictive.

Opiates are powerful. In prescription form, they are highly regulated yet continue to be misused and abused. Prescription opiates are sometimes snorted for a much quicker high, which increases the likelihood of death. Accidental overdose can also occur when prescription and street opiates are combined.

Pain Management Programs

Pain management programs may be inpatient or outpatient and consist of comprehensive and structured classes designed to help individuals who suffer from chronic pain. They are found in many hospitals and in some privately operated facilities and rehabilitation centers. The American Academy of Pain Management evaluates and accredits institutions and providers. Some pain management programs are more sensitive to addiction or the potential for addiction than others. Some emphasize medical management of pain and see their mission as the reduction of suffering by mostly medicinal means. Others emphasize psychological techniques, movement, breathing, physical therapy, and a blend of methods designed to assist in the reduction of pain and improved management of ongoing pain. Recently emerging are specialty pain management programs specifically designed for addicts or those with high addiction potential.

Most pain management programs embrace a comprehensive, multidisciplinary approach, but their emphasis and philosophy may vary. A comprehensive approach to pain management can radically improve one's quality of life.

Addiction as a Consequence of Pain Medication

Painkillers, typically opiates, prescribed for chronic pain due to a chronic illness, a serious accident, or surgery, are addictive. The number of chronic pain patients who become addicted to their pain medication is unknown, but it's not uncommon. In addition, many slowly developing addictions flourish when chronic pain develops. Following an injury, a social drinker may start drinking alcoholically. Using or drinking becomes a way of dealing with the loss of a job, sport, or other fulfilling experience.

When it comes to pain medication, some people take one or two pills and discard the rest. Those who have ongoing and debilitating pain continue to ingest the medication as necessary. A third category of people takes the drugs even when they are no longer necessary for physical pain. They like the way the drug makes them feel. In either of the latter two cases, addiction can result. How does the medical community determine whether to prescribe painkillers, and what are the risk factors?

Opinions vary with practitioners and institutions regarding the long-term use of opiates for managing chronic pain. Many people with chronic pain are dependent on opiates, yet not addicted. They use their medicines as prescribed, they are dependent upon them for pain relief, and if they stopped taking them, they would experience withdrawal. They do not, however, become obsessed about using or finding more medication or continue to use it despite negative consequences. The story is different for those whose prescription drug use causes them to cross the line into addiction: addicts, who will crave more of the drug, and addicts in recovery, who need to take extra measures of precaution to maintain their recovery and still manage their pain.

It is almost impossible to predict who will become addicted to pain medication. Doctors rely on information the patient and family members disclose, including any family history of addiction. The majority of doctors take great care not to overprescribe pain medication. In fact, some pain specialists say the fear of addicting people has resulted in too little pain medication being made available, especially with terminal illnesses and excruciating pain. Nobody should suffer needlessly, and those with addiction potential, or actual addiction history, may need to take extra precautions when dealing with a physical illness or injury requiring pain medicine. Prescription pain medication can be appropriately and safely used if managed by a trusted third party, such as a family member or sponsor. As long as someone else can manage access to the drug, and the prescription is time limited, painful medical situations can be handled safely.

Active Addicts and Pain Management

Up to 60 percent of emergency room visits involve injury associated with the consequences of drinking or drugging. Addicts are at higher risk than nonaddicts for injury and disease, and so they are also at risk for developing chronic pain. The number of addicts who develop chronic pain conditions is not clear, but it is likely higher than average. Addicts are also often suspected of creating factitious pain in order to secure narcotics.

When is pain manipulated and when is it real? Addicts can be master manipulators, so the question of whether a patient's pain is real or fabricated sometimes derails health care providers. Most people can mimic a condition if they know the symptoms to feign. Some individuals are motivated by or perhaps addicted to the attention more than the medicines. The faking, exaggeration, or creation of a medical condition in order to obtain attention, treatment, or sympathy is known as Munchausen syndrome. Some people with Munchausen syndrome are also addicts. However, most addicts who are seeking medication do so knowingly, not as a result of complex psychiatric conditions. Many of these individuals do have chronic pain but report unmanageable levels of pain in pursuit of their drug of choice.

We tend to see more than just addiction, just chronic pain, or just the two together. Very often, there is an intricate co-occurrence of multiple psychological, social, and perceptual factors that makes pain management more complex. Depression and anxiety are common with chronic pain.

Pain Management with Addicts in Recovery

One of the greater controversies in the pain management and addiction fields is how to treat a medical patient in pain who is in recovery from addiction. In the old days, addicts were advised to stay away from any and all pain medications. Many pain medications are addictive, and addicts in recovery, regardless of their drug of choice, are supposed to be abstinent—to stay drug free. Even onetime use can trigger the desire to use the drug of choice again. Early AA and NA underscored complete abstinence. If you had pain, you simply had to tough it out.

Modern thinking still emphasizes abstinence but is less extreme. It is becoming more commonly accepted that with preparation, most addicts can safely take a short-term course of pain medication and maintain recovery. Enlisting friends and family for support, informing physicians of the concerns, communicating more often with sponsors, and putting others in charge of dispensing the medication tend to work quite well. While these strategies may work for short-term management of severe pain, chronic pain raises more difficult problems. It is wise to use the shortest course of pain medication possible while aggressively introducing nonaddictive or natural methods of pain management. Biofeedback, physical therapy, exercise such as yoga, and over-the-counter analgesics can provide much relief.

Ultram, a synthetic opiate believed to be less addicting, is occasionally used for short-term severe pain management in addiction treatment centers. Some physicians see Darvocet as a milder pain medication, possibly less prone to abuse. Nonaddictive pain medications, such as antidepressants and anticonvulsants, can be prescribed for pain. Sometimes a patient on one form of antidepressant or anticonvulsant is given a higher dosage or additional medication. Although not painkillers, these medications affect the nerve pathways and the serotonin levels involved in the experience of pain. Newer anticonvulsant medications are becoming more widely used for management of nerve pain. Nonsteroidal anti-inflammatory medications, such as Motrin, Advil, or Tylenol, can often be safely used in addition to these medications, but patients should talk to their doctors and pharmacists first.

Treating the Active Addict Who Has Chronic Pain

The first challenge in treating the co-occurring disorder of chronic pain and addiction is addressing the addiction. If the pain is ignored or invalidated, however, the chances of relapse are high. In many instances, the program of recovery designed to help with addiction will help with the management of chronic pain. This may be part of the reason pain seems to diminish, and in some cases disappear, once the individual begins working a recovery program. Regardless of what happens to a patient's level of pain in recovery, do not assume that complaints of pain are (or were) efforts to secure more drugs.

If pain levels continue to be high during and after treatment, numerous effective techniques, technologies, and strategies are available that do not involve the use of opiates or other addictive medications. Legitimate, well-balanced pain management programs, usually recommended after completion of a drug treatment program, focus heavily on natural painkilling techniques, skill building, and changes in attitude. These methods are highly effective but require considerable work and follow-through. Ongoing involvement in addiction treatment, including Step work, is necessary for good outcomes. Some pain management programs include and advocate the Steps, but only a few actively combine addiction treatment and pain management. Patients can get good results with different levels of care for each disorder, outpatient for one and inpatient for the other, depending upon severity and chronicity of each condition. For the toughest cases, inpatient pain management should immediately follow inpatient drug treatment. The most complex cases might require both treatments combined.

Summary and Recommendations

If a loved one suffers from chronic pain and addiction, she may be at greater risk for additional co-occurring disorders. Addiction can happen before, during, or after chronic pain begins. Depression and anxiety tend to travel along with chronic pain and addiction. As with most co-occurring disorders, the core factors of psychology, belief systems, attitude, support systems, physical activity, and spirituality play a role in recovery. If you are convinced your loved one displays an addiction, not simply a dependence, consult with an addiction professional, mental health professional, interventionist, or addictionologist. Do not rely solely on the feedback of the physician prescribing the pain medicine that you believe may be problematic.

Select a primary drug treatment program or a program that treats chronic pain and addiction simultaneously. If addiction is part of the problem, select a drug treatment facility that will not immediately assume all pain is drug-seeking behavior. A far less common problem today, this used to be a bigger issue years ago. A quality provider will do a comprehensive physical evaluation and respect the reality of pain without feeding the addiction or victim mind-set. Validation is important. Confrontation without validation can easily backfire. The majority of primary treatment programs treat addicts who are in pain with dignity and respect.

Select a pain management program or set of providers. Coordinate inpatient or outpatient care to focus on nonaddictive pain management. Find a fully certified, multidisciplinary pain management practice, program, or center. Many programs blend conventional and alternative approaches. Combining physical rehabilitation, massage, imaging work, acupuncture, and other techniques is often desirable.

Learn more about pain management. The range and scope of pain management options are considerable. Learn about the various medication approaches, many of which are nonaddictive, and, more important, the wide range of medical and natural techniques that can dramatically improve quality of life.

Encourage your loved one to work on acceptance. Patients need to make peace with their pain; it is not the enemy. Most pain management experts agree that acceptance is one of the most important and difficult hurdles.

Encourage your loved one to address depression, anxiety, irrational thinking, sleep disturbances, and other emotional issues. As with all co-occurring psychological issues, a combination of medication and psychotherapy is advised. When dealing with pain management, attitude and psychological symptoms interact in a very intimate way. Managing emotions, perceptions, and attitudes is a vital part of pain management. Fatigue and emotional triggers can disrupt the best technique. Learn to recognize when attitude is slipping and what to do about it. Patients need to avoid isolation, inactivity, victim thinking, hopelessness, overeating, and self-loathing.

Encourage your loved one to work on managing thoughts, feelings, and urges. Bad days, painful days, and triggers will occur. Ongoing sobriety requires preparation and practice. Review materials on relapse prevention and apply them to pain as well. Patients can develop a clear system that is their own.

Encourage continuation of Twelve Step meetings and communicating with a sponsor. Patients can take on a chronic pain sponsor. They can easily find someone in a Twelve Step meeting who has to manage chronic pain. It is easier to trust and relate to someone who has similar challenges.

Your loved one needs to work on continuous self-care. Diet, exercise, routine, structure, and supports are all important components of self-care. Patients should confer with their doctors about appropriate levels of exercise within their physical limits. Working with a qualified physical therapist is strongly recommended. Those who deal with chronic pain should not push the limits and be mindful of pacing. They should stay active but avoid exhaustion. Patients may need support and guidance in safely working through stiffness, immobility, and pain. Finding the balance between pushing and pacing oneself is uniquely challenging for those who live with chronic pain.

Those in recovery who face severe pain daily may find it more challenging to experience serenity and the promises of recovery. Daily pain may also enhance cravings for mood-altering or pain-killing drugs. Self-pity is easily reignited, especially after a bad day. Spirituality includes gratitude and acceptance. Patients in chronic pain can celebrate their gifts, accept the reality of their physical condition, and recommit themselves to actively pursue strategies that help.

As with all co-occurring disorders, more effort in treatment and recovery may be required. The more committed the patient is to a comprehensive strategy for recovery and self-maintenance, the better the prospects. While it is not possible to make chronic pain, physical injury, or addiction disappear, working a solid program of self-care, in concert with rigorous application of nonaddictive pain management strategies, can result in a gratifying, sober, and productive existence. Pain can eventually become part of one's identity and be embraced with meaning and purpose. Being of service to others and encouraging those who are not as far along in the journey foster recovery in self and others.

Case History

Latisha, a thirty-four-year-old nurse, suffered from spina bifida. This disease had caused a gradual degeneration of her lower spinal column over the last eight years, causing her constant discomfort and pain. She had always worked hard to manage the illness, following the suggestions of her doctors.

Latisha had also been an accomplished swimmer since high school, helping her team at Detroit's Denby High School win the state championship. Although her disease was often agonizing, she found relief in swimming, which helped her to stretch and exercise her spine and to work the supporting muscles.

Latisha fought valiantly through her illness, raising two children with her husband, Dewayne. She had always avoided opiate painkillers, as her nursing background made her all too well aware of the dangers. In her work, she had seen many accidental addicts become dependent on prescription pain medication.

A new doctor suggested that Latisha try a new brand of narcotic painkiller when she was going through a particularly difficult period. At first, she used the medication as directed. But as time went by, she began increasing her dosage, and soon she learned how to order the pills over the Internet. The more she used the narcotics, the less interested she seemed in swimming; the less she swam, the more she relied upon the narcotic medication to control her pain. It was a prime example of a situation that Latisha had seen in other patients. She knew that taking more pills was making her more dependent and created a higher tolerance for the medication so she would need more medication to achieve the same effect. It was a vicious circle, and Latisha knew it, but she was unable to stop.

Dewayne confronted her about her growing dependence on the medication, but Latisha used her medical background as a buttress against his attacks, saying that he did not know enough to criticize her and accusing him of being unsympathetic. Over a period of eighteen months, Latisha's dependence worsened, and she began taking more and more time off work. She blamed this on the spina bifida, but in fact her absences were caused by her addiction. She was often unwilling to get out of bed, help with child care, or go to her job at the hospital. She used up all her sick time, as well as her vacation time, within the first five months of the new year.

Finally, it became necessary for Dewayne and the rest of her family to mount an intervention. With the help of a professional, they began their preparations, including travel arrangements for Latisha's favorite aunt to fly in from Memphis. The plan was to confront Latisha with love and concern and to get her the help she needed.

Working with the interventionist, the family chose a medically intensive treatment center that worked closely with a well-known pain management clinic. Latisha's treatment plan would require her detoxification from the narcotics, along with a comprehensive strategy for addressing her pain. The nature of her illness was such that her spinal cord was deteriorating, but not at such a rate that she would become immobilized.

From a natural pain management standpoint, her old swimming regimen would be one of the best tools at her disposal. The combination of exercise and gentle stretching would be perfect for helping to keep her spinal disease in check. In addition, over-the-counter drugs such as ibuprofen or acetaminophen (Advil or Tylenol) would be nearly as effective as narcotics in helping to control the pain. Their anti-inflammatory properties would also be beneficial.

A crisis developed prior to the intervention when one family member inadvertently included Latisha in an e-mail exchange about the upcoming intervention, and so Latisha knew of her family's plans prior to intervention day. This situation can be problematic, as it will often cause addicted people to avoid the intervention. Latisha lashed out at her husband, accusing him of abandoning her in her time of need. But he refused to be drawn into an argument and instead drew her into his arms. He explained that the family had found some new alternatives for her, and they were eager to share their knowledge. Latisha reluctantly agreed to attend the intervention.

More than a dozen family members were present when she came into her parents' living room. Their letters were brimming with love and admiration, along with a heartfelt request for her to accept help. Latisha was initially resistant to the idea, but she eventually agreed, under the relentless concern of her family.

Latisha had a long and difficult withdrawal, lasting more than seven days. It was nearly impossible for her to remain in the treatment program for two reasons. First, she desperately wanted to return to her narcotic medication; and, second, she didn't identify with the other patients, who had come to their addiction in a seemingly more voluntary fashion.

Over time, however, Latisha broke free of her physical dependence. At the same time, she came to realize that she wasn't so different from the other patients. After all, she was a registered nurse and she knew full well the addictive nature of the drugs she was prescribed. She also knew how dangerous it was to exceed the recommended dosage. Was she really so different from the alcoholic secretary?

After treatment, Latisha continued with the pain management clinic and resumed her old swimming routine. She also became involved in an aftercare group for health care professionals. These specialized groups cater to the needs of doctors, nurses, and other practitioners who have access to medications. Because they are licensed by the state, health care professionals require rigorous monitoring during their early recovery. This monitoring increases compliance with treatment and leads to higher success rates in long-term recovery.

Latisha is now back to swimming, back to nursing, and back to being a mother and wife. Her spina bifida will always be a factor in her life, but she has been able to apply the spirituality of the Twelve Steps to that problem as well.

"I'm powerless over the fact that I have spina bifida," says Latisha, "so I don't waste time feeling sorry for myself. I do what I need to do, and I get on with my life. Sure, I feel pain, but at least I'm not feeling the pain of addiction anymore."

13

Core Concepts for Treating Co-occurring Disorders

In the preceding chapters, we have provided you with information that can help you and your loved one on the journey to recovery. While each co-occurring disorder is different, there are common threads.

Complexity

Take two complicated problems, put them together, and you get a situation with even higher levels of complexity. This is what happens with co-occurring disorders. Co-occurring disorders are almost always complicated, but they are also highly treatable. Interventions and treatments that address both sets of problems are essential. In order to simplify things and manage the complexity, consider the following suggestions:

1. Avoid the seduction of a single solution. Addicts tend to look for the "easier, softer way." They attempt to deal with anxiety, depression, loneliness, confusion, and a long list of other symptoms by using chemicals. Others seek out unhealthy or addictive relationships. Some use food; others use video games. The tendency is toward single answers, and families get caught up in this as well. "John will be better as soon as he finds a good girlfriend." Simple, single solutions are easy to buy into

but usually just become a means of distraction and avoidance. Addicts, especially those with co-occurring conditions, are masters of manipulation—of themselves, primarily, and their families as well.

2. Complex problems need multidisciplinary treatment. Treating one condition or set of conditions without including the others is a setup for disaster. On occasion, some individuals "get lucky"—AA provides someone enough support that a minor depression self-corrects, or a depressed person may decide she no longer needs to drink once her depression is successfully treated— but all too often, especially with addicted individuals, multiple and simultaneous treatments are needed and required. Comprehensive, multidisciplinary treatment, at the proper level of care, is required. Don't settle for less.

The Four Dimensions

Here's a simple rule: The more severe the addiction or psychological impairment in a co-occurring disorder, the greater the damage to the four dimensions, and the more important that the interventions, treatments, and levels of care match the damage. More than just medicine is usually needed, and addressing all four dimensions is a must.

The four dimensions have been referred to in earlier chapters. They are

1. Biological: Medical attention, including psychiatric medicine when needed, diet, and exercise, is a necessary part of recovery.

2. Psychological: Individual and/or group psychotherapy can be invaluable in helping shift the perceptions and belief systems of those dealing with co-occurring disorders. The research literature and our clinical experience reinforce this wisdom. (AA's originators, too,

strongly recommended psychological and psychiatric care and did not see it as negative.)

3. Interpersonal: Changes in peer groups are vital. Overcoming feelings of uniqueness and ending isolation and negative peer influence are potent healing factors.

4. Spiritual: Direct or indirect challenges to core belief systems can be important. Addressing this highest level of thinking need not be formal or religious. However, interventions and challenges at this level can make a huge difference. This is the battleground of hope and hopelessness. Giving up, or at least lessening, one's negative belief systems facilitates healing and creates possibilities. This is applicable to both addiction and psychological disorders.

Top Down, Bottom Up

Utilizing all four dimensions adheres to the simple principle of "top down" and "bottom up" mentioned in chapter 3. We now know that higher-order interventions—cognitive and spiritual—have a powerful effect on the brain and body. Similarly, there is very strong evidence that bottom-up factors—diet, exercise, and medicine—affect thinking, decision making, and behavior. Addressing all four factors means you are addressing co-occurring issues from both directions: top down and bottom up.

Simplify and Accept

"It is what it is" and "Accept life on life's terms" sound like clichés. However, they are vital parts of recovering from co-occurring disorders. Perfectionism, denial, and fantasy are all fueled by co-occurring conditions. Working on acceptance is key to letting go of illusion and distraction. A good treatment program and comprehensive treatment facilitate a more realistic view of what the problems in a disorder are. Most often they are not nearly as dire as feared, or as minor as hoped. Accepting the addiction and psychological conditions is a vital first step in working on recovery. Chasing complex aspects and consequences of the disorder(s) wastes time and resources. Older models encouraged insight prior to change. This is no longer considered necessary or valid. Recovery is an ongoing and active process, one that is fueled by changes in behavior, not simply insight. Recovery begins when those afflicted can see problems realistically and honestly instead of through a veil of denial, pretending they don't exist. As the AA program states: "Progress, not perfection." Or as Dr. Boriskin advises his patients: "Grieve the ideal, celebrate the real." For addicts, that might mean never drinking or smoking pot again. In an ideal world, they could, without consequence. But the alternative, the reality of sobriety, is quite positive and requires simple acceptance. Similarly, embracing one's depression and engaging in treatment is a more positive approach than simply wishing it would go away.

Sequence Is Vital

The most effective order of treatment is to start with the addiction, then immediately address the psychological issues. Treating disorders out of sequence can undermine the recovery from both. Being drug and alcohol free is essential if the psychological condition is to be treated successfully. Progress will not take place until the chemical use is out of the picture. Also, delaying psychological treatment when a patient is newly sober, which used to be the recommendation a couple of decades ago, is most often wrong. The sooner the psychological issues are addressed in early recovery, the better the prognosis for both disorders.

Seek a Precise Diagnosis

Some psychological disorders are difficult to diagnose. As we learned in chapter 6, bipolar disorders are particularly difficult. If your loved one continues to relapse, or has problems that persist, it is possible that the correct diagnosis has not yet been derived. Seek additional testing and second opinions. Look for what has been overlooked. Sometimes additional, sophisticated testing can have profound results.

Do Not Chase the Hole in the Sidewalk

Some symptomatic individuals delay getting treatment or making necessary changes until they know "all the answers." The hole in the sidewalk is a metaphor that illustrates this—you can begin fixing the hole even if you don't know how it got there. Searching for complete understanding before making behavioral changes is common with both addiction and psychological problems. While pursuit of a correct diagnosis is important, waiting until the explanation is found before behaviors change can slow down recovery or even stop treatment from starting. You do not need to know exactly why your tooth hurts before you go to the dentist. Do not be paralyzed by an impossible quest for complete explanation before an action plan and treatment begin. Do not confuse an excuse with an explanation.

One Condition Excusing the Other

People with co-occurring disorders sometimes think, "I will stop drinking once I am no longer depressed," or " I don't need help for my depression as long as I am no longer drinking." But co-occurring conditions can "feed" off of one another just like this. But do not be manipulated by one condition excusing the other. They both need attention: The addiction should be treated first, and the psychological disorder should be addressed once the addiction treatment is under way.

Patience, Not Passivity

Recovery takes time, effort, and patience. Behavioral changes, patterns of behavior, and addictive disorders do not change suddenly. Treatment is a start, but recovery is a process. As they say in the program, "Time takes time." Also, relapse is more likely with co-occurring disorders. Do not be devastated by this, but do not delay in intervention. Look upon a relapse not as a failure but as an opportunity for learning and refinement. Do not abandon recovery or give up on a loved one simply because of a relapse. Patience is required. However, passivity when someone remains symptomatic is a different story. Waiting for "spontaneous" insight or change in a person or waiting for a person to "grow" out of using can be a dangerous illusion. Indeed, it is very, very difficult to distinguish between passivity and patience. That is where outside support and guidance can be invaluable.

Reframe

Let go of blame and shame. Rather than getting angry at yourself or your loved one, stay angry at the problem. Let your anger mobilize you toward effective action, not poisonous frustration. As a simple yet profound saying goes, "The problem is the problem." Get your ego and pride out of the equation. Addiction is treatable; abstinence is needed. Most psychological conditions are treatable; they take time and effort. Some require more effort than others, and some conditions disappear, while others are lifelong. Quality of life can be reclaimed. It takes commitment, work, and multi-disciplinary action in all four core areas mentioned previously—biological, psychological, interpersonal, and spiritual. Progress, not perfection, is the goal.

Recommendations for Families and Loved Ones

Take Action

When dealing with a co-occurring disorder, it's important to confront the problem, but love the person. Many families facing a co-occurring disorder become paralyzed by fear, perhaps manipulated into silence. But a great deal of damage is done by allowing the disorders to rule without challenge. Taking action has many meanings, and each situation requires careful consideration and planning. The first action—the seeking of knowledge—is taken simply by reading this book. Knowledge is empowering and gives you choices, not perfect answers. Consider what interventions may help and what resources you need to implement a plan of change. Learn more about specific disorders, their treatments, and the medications involved. Action can have negative consequences if poorly done or mistimed, but inaction tends to take the larger toll, at least from our observations. Loved ones have much, much more power than they think. With knowledge, professional guidance, and support, good outcomes can happen. A final note: Action does not mean confrontation and hostility. In fact, confrontation should only take the form of a loving discussion or intervention. This is a skill that most often requires support and outside assistance.

Seek Support

Your loved one's condition puts stress upon the entire family. This stress affects judgment, objectivity, clarity, serenity, and decision making. Without support, family members often become more extreme; they may give in more frequently or become enraged. This is a normal stress response. In fact, black-and-white thinking is a predictable response to external stress. However, it is most often nonproductive and sometimes highly damaging. Families need additional voices and support. They can get this in many ways: through individual therapy, psychiatric consultation, medication, family therapy, and active participation in support groups. The more stress family members encounter, the more effort and resources they might need to expend to deal with the stress. Co-occurring disorders affect and infect everyone. Do not sacrifice your own needs or wait for your loved one to spontaneously get well. Also, being a martyr or becoming symptomatic yourself will not shock your loved one into getting better. The stronger and more supported you are, the more likely your input will be effective, balanced, and meaningful. This does not guarantee a positive outcome, but it does enhance effectiveness and improve the odds. It is vital that you manage your emotional assets wisely. It is a definite requirement in the journey of recovery.

Be Assertive

If your intuition says that not all factors have been identified or are being addressed, ask questions of providers and/or seek other opinions. If your loved one is not getting better, consider other providers, other agencies, or higher levels of care. This does not mean becoming angry, demanding, or impatient. Instead, we encourage you to become assertive. Quality providers welcome assertive, logical questions as part of information exchange. You may have observations, family history facts, or specific concerns that your loved one—their patient—has not communicated. Read "Navigating the Maze" in chapter 2 (pages 20–22) and advocate that all four core dimensions of recovery—biological, psychological, interpersonal, and spiritual—are addressed. Participate in family programs and seek and provide as much information as you can, while still respecting healthy boundaries and limits of confidentiality.

Learn about Codependency

Codependency is a complicated and controversial topic. However, its core concepts are highly applicable to co-occurring disorders. Perhaps the strongest concept revolves around the four Cs: (1) Cause—you didn't cause it, even though you might have been a contributor; (2) Cure—you cannot cure it, but you can make a contribution to recovery; (3) Control—you do not have control, but you have (4) Choices and conditions—you can choose how you allocate your resources. It is not wrong to place conditions on certain behaviors; for example, making it clear that you will only provide financial support to a loved one if he remains abstinent.

Apply the Core Concepts to Yourself As Well

The journey toward recovery is arduous and sometimes lengthy. Self-care is vital, and you need to address the four core dimensions required for your own self-care. Staying healthy empowers you. Getting sick along with your loved one diminishes you and feeds the illness.

Speak the Languages

Addiction and mental health providers speak slightly different languages and emphasize different but equally valid aspects of treatment and recovery. Do not become overwhelmed by the language. The vocabulary is not as intimidating as it might first appear, but do not hesitate to ask questions. If the provider cannot explain elements of the disorder and treatment options with clarity, seek other opinions.

Language also applies to the internal dialogue of addiction and psychological disorders. Many times these "languages" are identical, but on some occasions the language of the addiction is distinctly different. Try to address both possibilities as you learn more about the conditions. For example, procrastination about getting a job might be the result of the internal language of depression, hopelessness, and despair, typical feelings associated with psychological disorders. But at the same time, the internal addict might be whispering that inactivity allows an opportunity to keep using. Building your language skills is a process, requiring flexibility and time. As your loved one gets better, her internal languages will become healthier.

Maintain and Communicate Positive Expectations

Both addiction and psychological disorders, especially when co-occurring, tend to rob everyone of hope. We strongly urge a positive outlook, even during the most trying times. When your loved one is most symptomatic, he might want to pull you into the "abyss." Do not go there. Hold on to your own vision, one of hope and recovery. It is good for you and good for your loved one.

When dealing with co-occurring disorders, we have to think differently than if we were dealing with only one issue at a time.

When we blend psychological problems with addiction, things can get complex, but with the right mind-set, amazing results are attainable. We hope this book is the beginning of that right mind-set. In the preceding chapters, we have described the foundations of what you and your loved one will need. It is not a simple or easy journey, but it can and does work.

14

The Twelve Steps
and Co-occurring Disorders

The greatest obstacle to successfully treating any kind of chronic illness is compliance—getting patients to follow the directions. Whether the problem is alcoholism, heart disease, or diabetes, there is no shortage of effective treatments. But most patients simply don't follow their treatment plans.

Recovery from chronic illnesses often requires that patients make profound changes in their lives, often around diet and exercise, that can be hard to sustain. Heart disease provides a clear example.

A friend of ours, Bob, suffered a heart attack a few years ago. He received immediate treatment and survived. The next day, his cardiologist came to speak with him.

"Bob," he said, "you're a very lucky man. There's been almost no damage to your heart. If you change your diet, increase your exercise, and take the medication I'm going to prescribe, you'll probably never have a second heart attack."

"I like the sound of that," said Bob. "It sounds pretty simple."

"Simple, yes," said the doctor. "But most people won't do it."

"Really?"

"You'd be amazed how many people hear this little speech and then wind up back in the hospital with a second heart attack," said the doctor. "That is, if they survive the second heart attack."

"Sobering," said Bob.

"Which brings up a good point," said the doctor. "I know you're a recovering alcoholic, Bob, and that may be a great asset to you now."

"How so?" asked Bob.

"I think you've got a better chance of following through because you've learned to follow directions to the letter. For example, your sobriety demands that you not drink alcohol. Ever. It doesn't mean 50 percent of the time or 95 percent of the time; it means that you follow your program and you don't drink alcohol 100 percent of the time."

"That's what recovery is all about," said Bob. "And it's a better life too."

"If you can apply the same principles to heart disease that you've used in dealing with your alcoholism," said the doctor, "you'll be a great success."

"I'll do it."

And he did. It's been a number of years now since Bob had his heart attack, and not only has he been free of heart problems, but at age sixty-three, he's in the best shape of his life.

"I had to have the same spiritual awakening around diet and exercise as I did around drinking," said Bob, looking back on his heart attack. "It's what made it possible for me to keep following the directions every day."

Alcoholics Anonymous and other Twelve Step programs provide a recipe for a spiritual awakening that isn't dependent on religious belief. Twelve Step programs provide the best, most time-tested road map to long-term recovery.

There is an old saying in AA: "Recovery is easy. You just have to change everything." And when a person has to make global changes in life, it requires an awakening of spirit that is great enough to meet the challenge. Recovery from alcoholism or drug addiction, like recovery from mental health issues, requires the full participation of body, mind, and spirit. It isn't a matter of taking a pill and waiting for the problem to go away. In fact, most of the printed directions that accompany prescription medications for anxiety and depression suggest that patients engage in therapy and ongoing support.

Spiritual awakening does not mean religious conversion. In fact, one of the reasons that the Twelve Steps in the book *Alcoholics Anonymous*—the Big Book—have been so widely studied is that they provide a prescription for this awakening that doesn't require formal religion. If one has religious faith, that is all well and good, but the program works equally as well for agnostics and atheists. The Big Book contains a chapter called "We Agnostics," which addresses this issue in a personal and practical way.

What the Twelve Step program does call for is that people identify something greater than themselves to serve as a guiding light. This may be truth, moral principles, or a universal power. Or it may be God *as they understand God*, whether through formal religion, personal faith, or both. The Twelve Steps make no judgment in these matters. People must decide what they believe for themselves. For many people, the process of questioning and discovering what they really believe can serve as a spiritual awakening.

Alcoholics who participate in Twelve Step meetings regularly are willing to change their lives for the better. They have the opportunity to learn from people who have successfully overcome similar problems. They are able to draw on the counsel of more experienced members. Because there are no fees for Twelve Step meetings, and because help is freely offered by those who have firsthand experience with recovery, this counsel is often perceived by newcomers as being more valuable than the same advice given by professionals.

The actions of going to meetings on a regular basis, of not drinking or using drugs, of working with a sponsor (or mentor), and of reading recovery literature begin a new routine and a new sense of responsibility. This new responsibility is not aimed at a person or institution, but rather at the health and well-being of the individuals themselves so they can begin to reclaim their lives.

For people dealing with co-occurring disorders, this new sense of responsibility extends beyond a typical addiction treatment and aftercare plan to include the specific steps they need to take to address their mental health issues. Instead of discontinuing their prescribed medication simply because they "didn't feel like taking it," patients continue to follow directions. Instead of quitting aftercare treatment because they are bored with it, they will persevere because their actions are in line with a Higher Power or higher principle rather than passing whims.

Participating in a Twelve Step group provides long-term structure and guidance, functional and healthy peer groups, and a chance to help others. It may seem counterintuitive that people with problems would need to help others, but let's examine the facts and try to understand this important point.

People recovering from dual disorders are often discouraged and depressed. They aren't sure how to escape their dilemma, so they sink deeper and deeper into despair. Once they participate in a program of recovery over a course of time, they can draw on their firsthand experience and assure newcomers that it's okay to be uncertain, that no one will expect them to get better overnight, and that they'll be accepted. They can help make newcomers feel as if they belong in the group. Feeling accepted, newcomers return and can begin to heal. Here is an example of how this process can work.

Carmen, age thirty-three, has completed treatment for alcoholism and bipolar disorder. She is back home living with her husband and looking for a new job. She is going to AA on a daily basis, including an all-women's meeting three times per week. After a month, her sponsor recommends that she volunteer as a greeter to welcome newcomers. The next week, a new woman comes to the meeting. Her name is Nicole and she is only twenty-three. Like Carmen, she has recently completed treatment, but she isn't sure she wants to go to meetings.

"Welcome," says Carmen, reaching out to shake her hand.

"I don't exactly want to be here," says Nicole, looking away.

"I know what you mean," says Carmen. "I didn't exactly come here to meet people, if you know what I mean."

Nicole laughs and shakes hands. They start talking a bit as they walk into the meeting room. Carmen is too new to give advice, but she knows she doesn't have to. Nicole just needs someone to listen to her and introduce her to the other women. Carmen makes the introductions and shares some of her own story as well.

"I just went off the deep end," says Carmen. "It was booze and pills and the bipolar stuff. My husband was ready to leave me. But since I got back from treatment, things seem to be working out. But still, we have a long way to go."

"You don't look like you were that messed up," says Nicole.

"Well, I wasn't wearing a sign on my forehead," Carmen says with a smile.

They both laugh and keep talking, and when the meeting begins, the women sit together. At the end of the meeting, Nicole speaks to the whole group.

"I was nervous coming here tonight, but my new friend Carmen met me at the door and introduced me to all of you, and I just can't thank her enough. She made me feel so comfortable. I think you'll see me here again."

Hearing these words said aloud to a group of women she respects will make Carmen feel better than anything else could. In a few short minutes, giving a little of herself to a stranger, she stepped into a new world. Now, Carmen's own tale of addiction, mental illness, and recovery will become a benefit to someone else. Her greatest defects have a chance to become her greatest assets. She will be able to listen and talk with Nicole like few others in Nicole's life, because Carmen is a recovering addict herself.

People often talk about building self-esteem, but there is really only one way to do it. We must do things that we can respect. If we accomplish things we can be proud of consistently, then we will build a solid base of self-esteem. In our example above, Carmen found she had something unique to give. She has always respected people who helped other people, but she never imagined she could do it herself, particularly with her own problems. Imagine the awakening of Carmen's heart and spirit when she discovered she could be the one to reach out a helping hand.

In previous chapters, we talked at length about the need to develop new and healthy peers when dealing with mental health problems. Here is the perfect opportunity. We have also talked about the need to find appropriate support and to be able to talk through problems with family and friends. Here are the friends, and they may well understand more than the family. We have also discussed the need to find strong internal motivation and purpose to work through the difficulties of recovery from mental illnesses. Here is the method for developing that motivation and purpose.

The Twelve Steps have helped millions of people in more than one hundred countries since the inception of AA in 1935, yet some people question the efficacy of the Twelve Step approach. People point out that AA is not evidence-based medicine, that it has not been subjected to the kind of rigorous double-blind studies (studies that ensure that neither the researcher nor the subject knows what treatments are being used) required by modern researchers. This is partially true. The Steps were not developed as a result of evidence-based research, but that concept didn't exist in 1935 with respect to psychology. On the other hand, AA Twelve Step–based treatment has been studied thoroughly. The National Institute on Alcohol Abuse and Alcoholism (NIAAA) and many other institutions have conducted double-blind studies and found AA to be unsurpassed in the treatment of alcoholism. The landmark "Project Match" study by NIAAA provides a good example.

There are those who say AA is a religious program. People of many religions, as well as atheists and agnostics, attend AA meetings, but there is no religious dogma in any Twelve Step literature. While it's true that the Steps mention the word *God*, they do not refer to God in any dogmatic or systematic way, which is required in order to be religious. AA literature is consistent in stating that individuals must work out the idea of God for themselves. By contrast, religion presents a specific set of beliefs, or dogma. Some people say AA is not religious enough, but the fact is that Twelve Step programs encourage their members to search out and develop their own beliefs.

Some critics also say that going to meetings frequently is like a substitute addiction, and it somehow undercuts the free will of the individual by substituting a kind of "groupthink." But there is nothing unusual about devoting an hour a day to any new pursuit, especially one that requires a lifestyle change. A rigorous diet and weight-loss plan would require at least that much time. For someone who has quit using drugs or alcohol, finding an hour a day is very easy. Indeed, one of the principal problems in early recovery is filling the hours that used to be devoted to intoxication. AA provides a way to do this in a healthy manner.

Many offshoots of the original Twelve Step groups of Alcoholics Anonymous have developed over the years to address a wide range of issues. These include Narcotics Anonymous, Cocaine Anonymous, Al-Anon (for the family members of alcoholics), Emotions Anonymous (for mental health issues), Food Addicts Anonymous, Gamblers Anonymous, Sex Addicts Anonymous, Families Anonymous, and many more. All these groups use the Steps with only slight modification to address their focal area.

Alcoholics Anonymous began in 1935, and when the fledgling organization grew to one hundred sober alcoholics (in 1939), they decided to try to write down the steps they had taken to achieve sobriety. Long-term recovery from alcoholism was a foreign idea at that time, and they wanted to capture in words what they had done to accomplish this feat. That is why the Steps are written in the past tense, because this is what the individuals had done to achieve sobriety. It is also why they are written in the plural form, from the point of view of "we." For people in recovery, "we" can be a very important concept, because isolation often leads to relapse.

So what are the Twelve Steps of AA? We will take a brief look at them, try to bring a little clarity to the program, and suggest how the Steps are applicable to mental health problems. (The Steps have been slightly modified by groups such as Dual Recovery Anonymous, but their essence remains the same.) A more complete introduction to the Steps can be found in the book *Twelve Steps and Twelve Traditions*, published by Alcoholics Anonymous.

Step One: We admitted we were powerless over alcohol—
that our lives had become unmanageable.

The admission by alcoholics that they have a problem is the necessary beginning point of recovery. With addiction and mental health issues, this is especially important because denial is a primary feature of the illnesses. So people with co-occurring disorders must state in a clear and unambiguous manner that they have a problem and it is damaging their lives.

People have sometimes misunderstood the use of the word *powerless* to mean that the alcoholic cannot help but drink and has no personal responsibility in the matter. The *Big Book*, and many volumes of recovery literature, makes it crystal clear that *powerless* refers to the inability to control drinking once the drinking has begun. Step One is an admission that all attempts at controlled drinking have ultimately failed and that the drinking life has become unmanageable.

The concept of powerlessness can be very negative for survivors of abuse, oppression, and trauma. For those who have trauma-based difficulties, the concept of powerlessness may be either terrifying or just plain unacceptable. But Step One focuses entirely on addiction and does not extend to issues other than the use of mood-altering substances, as real as they might be. Powerlessness is restricted to the realm of addiction.

The most important action in Step One is admitting there is a problem. Overcoming denial is a central issue in both addiction and mental illness. By taking Step One, dually diagnosed patients put denial behind them and begin moving into the solution. Of course, denial can creep back from time to time, and that is why the continuing admission of Step One is so important.

Step Two: Came to believe that a Power greater than ourselves could restore us to sanity.

Albert Einstein said, "The brain that has the problem cannot solve the problem." Many people with co-occurring disorders struggle for years trying to find a solution to the problem within themselves and fail repeatedly. Step Two defines a new and more successful strategy. It says that the power to be restored to sanity will come from outside the individual. Step Two describes the all-important experience of "coming to believe" that this help is available and that it will work. It is often said that "God works through people." Alcoholics Anonymous and other Twelve Step programs demonstrate this fact every day. For people who have difficulty with a spiritual point of view, the concept of help coming from other people, from outside the self, is still powerful. The most important point of Step Two is that people come to believe that relief is possible, that they don't have to have all the answers, and that they can be restored to health and wholeness (the root meaning of the word *sanity*, from the Latin *sanus*).

If this can be tied to a belief in God or a Higher Power, the process may be easier. However, many recovering people have trouble in this area, and so they must search out their beliefs to find out what is important to them. This quest for meaning can be all-encompassing, and it gives added dimension to the recovery process.

For people with co-occurring disorders, there is often a lack of faith or an outright anger at God for their afflictions. The resolution of these issues, often over time, provides a solid basis for recovery. Note that the Step says "came to believe," not "believed." It is a process, not a foregone conclusion.

Step Three: Made a decision to turn our will and our lives over to the care of God as we understood Him.

The authors of the Big Book added italics at the end of Step Three—*as we understood Him*—to underscore the personal nature of faith and belief. AA does not dictate the faith or the belief. Rather, each person must discover and accept his own belief in his own way. For people new to recovery, clarifying their beliefs and living by them are essential.

For people suffering from addiction and mental health problems, the subject of free will is loaded with contradictions. We all have free will, but in the disease of addiction, free will is perverted and made to serve the illness. It is not free will that drives a person to the liquor store at 9 a.m. or to the crack house with the rent money. It is craving. It is not free will that decides to quit medication and therapy; it is the brain disease.

People recovering from mental health and addiction problems know from experience that they must hitch their wagon to a new star. A new decision must be made. They must stop turning their will and their lives over to addiction and mental illness. Instead, they must make a leap of faith and entrust themselves to a Higher Power—God, *as they understand God.*

Step Three does not say that alcoholics turn their lives and their wills over to God, because this is not possible with free will. Rather, the Step urges a person to turn her will over to the "care of God," to make her will congruent with God's will. For agnostics or atheists in Twelve Step programs, the concept of God has sometimes been changed to G.O.D.: Good Orderly Direction or Group of Drunks. In other words, they have made their ideals and the fellowship of AA their Higher Power.

But there is no need to be too abstract. For many alcoholics, Step Three is as simple as this statement: "I'm going to do what I'm supposed to do, instead of what I want to do. Tonight, that means I'm going to an AA meeting instead of a bar."

Step Four: Made a searching and fearless moral inventory of ourselves.
Step Five: Admitted to God, to ourselves, and to another human being the exact nature of our wrongs.

These two Steps naturally go together. In fact, many people in recovery talk about "completing a good Fourth and Fifth Step." It is one of the great milestones in early sobriety.

Recovery demands rigorous honesty, and because of the nature of addiction and mental illness, this has often been in short supply. One of the surest ways to build this new foundation of truthfulness is to be completely honest about the past. The inventory should be done in writing and with the guidance of a sponsor. The first three Steps will not last long without honesty, and one of the chief reasons for relapse is a failure to do a thorough Fourth and Fifth Step.

It is hard to write the inventory, but it is even harder to admit all of these wrongs to another human being. It can be a wrenching experience, but it paves the way for a healthy sense of humility and humanity and opens the door to learning, growth, and change.

Step Six: Were entirely ready to have God remove all these defects of character.
Step Seven: Humbly asked Him to remove our shortcomings.

Once the Fourth and Fifth Steps have been completed, newly recovering people are faced with their shortcomings. Typically, they must come to grips with the fact that they've been selfish, self-centered, angry, irresponsible, or resentful. These "defects of character" must be addressed, and the Twelve Steps suggest a method for resolving them. The idea here is that selfish people aren't going to bring an end to their own selfishness. Instead, a Higher Power must be employed to get the job done. Rather than confront these defects of character with pure willpower, a spiritual approach is suggested. It is interesting to note that an entire Step is devoted to getting "ready" to have these defects removed. Family members of people with co-occurring disorders will recognize this stubbornness right away. It should be noted that the concept of being ready to do these things is not the same as being comfortable with doing them. Humility and readiness often come from a realization that nothing else has worked and that change is necessary. People in treatment and early recovery are urged to cultivate this kind of readiness.

Step Eight: Made a list of all persons we had harmed, and became willing to make amends to them all.

Step Nine: Made direct amends to such people wherever possible, except when to do so would injure them or others.

These are two more Steps that naturally go together. They recall the old maxim "actions speak louder than words." Debts must be paid, apologies must be made, and wrongs must be righted wherever possible. In taking the actions laid out by these Steps, people start to feel good about themselves for a very simple reason: They are doing things that they themselves can respect. It is impossible to build up self-esteem simply by talking about it. Action is necessary, and in Steps Eight and Nine, people begin taking actions that lead to greater self-sufficiency and self-satisfaction.

It is ironic that people have criticized Twelve Step groups as absolving people of responsibility. These Steps show how important it is to take concrete action to address past wrongs. When people talk about "working the program," they are referring to all Twelve Steps and not just those that can be accomplished mentally.

Step Ten: Continued to take personal inventory and when we were wrong promptly admitted it.

Steps Ten, Eleven, and Twelve are often called the maintenance Steps. They are meant to reinforce the work that's been done and to prevent backsliding. Nowhere is this as evident as in Step Ten.

The prompt admission of any wrongs is a clear signal to the rest of the world that a recovering person is trying to live his life on a new basis. How often has the dually diagnosed individual tried to cover up in the past? How often has he lied? In Step Ten, people are urged to maintain a close watch on their behavior and to be truthful in all their activities.

Step Eleven: Sought through prayer and meditation to improve our conscious contact with God as we understood Him, praying only for knowledge of His will for us and the power to carry that out.

People who have been successful in recovery strive to improve. In Step Eleven, this striving is aimed at improving knowledge and understanding of a Higher Power and at gaining the strength to do what is right. Prayer and meditation are presented as the principal tools for this job, although for an agnostic or atheist, this will be limited to meditation or reflection. But by this stage of their development, newly recovering people will have resolved the God dilemma in their own personal way. Step Eleven is a universal prescription for spiritual growth and presents the essence of recovery in one sentence. It assumes the need for improvement and thus the existence of shortcomings. It proposes a Higher Power as the agent of change, instead of the individual. It helps to take people with co-occurring disorders outside themselves and provides them with a greater purpose and a method for attaining that purpose. It mentally directs people away from the negativity of their illnesses and into a positive vision of their lives. Finally, it directs people to a higher calling and a greater vision of themselves.

Step Twelve: Having had a spiritual awakening as the result of these steps, we tried to carry this message to alcoholics, and to practice these principles in all our affairs.

In our earlier example of Carmen volunteering to be a greeter at the AA meeting, we see how the message is usually carried. Twelve Step groups often say they are "programs of attraction, not promotion," so there is no proselytizing or public advertisements. These programs have worked well for decades, and their success speaks for itself.

It's not hard to imagine how a person would have a spiritual awakening after having gone through the process of admission, inventory, making amends, and so on. It is a practical method for changing a person's life. The first one hundred men and women to get sober stated in Step Twelve that they wanted to practice the principles of honesty, openness, and willingness in every aspect of their lives. "We are not saints," says a well-known passage from the Big Book. "The point is, that we are willing to grow along spiritual lines."

Given what we have written in previous chapters, it is easy to see how this process will benefit people dealing with mental health problems as well. The initial Steps of the program are a recipe for the kind of awakening required to make great changes. When working Step One, a person lays the groundwork for honesty by admitting the nature of the problem. It can be modified in a person's mind, for example, to say "I'm powerless over my depression, and it's made my life unmanageable." Steps Two and Three move from the problem to the solution: a Power greater than oneself. For depression, this may mean medication and treatment in addition to the traditional methods we discussed. Most important, it means following through and doing what one is supposed to do—positive action—instead of what one wants to do—negative action. The inventory and confession of Steps Four and Five could be helpful to anyone, but they are essential to someone in therapy and can help to deepen the therapeutic process as greater levels of honesty are attained.

Just like exercise equipment, the Twelve Steps don't work on their own or without effort. From time to time, we will hear a family member say, "She went to AA, but it didn't work." But we know that the wisdom of the old-timers in AA is more to the point: "It works if you work it."

We believe that if addiction is present with mental health problems, an appropriate Twelve Step group should be part of any treatment and aftercare plan. There may be exceptions to this rule, but they are highly unusual.

A paranoid schizophrenic who was recovering in AA made the following remarks: "When I stop going to meetings, it means I'm going to stop taking my medication. When I stop taking my medication, I start hallucinating, and all hell breaks loose. The next thing I know, someone is tying me to a gurney and putting me in a locked ward. So today, I'll go to a meeting."

Whether the problem is depression, anxiety, bipolar disorder, or any of the many mental health diagnoses, the support of a Twelve Step group will help with treatment plan compliance and long-term recovery.

Some people who are dually diagnosed have not always felt comfortable at AA meetings because they had different issues they needed to discuss. While it's true that a minority of AA meetings won't welcome a discussion of co-occurring disorders, most are very open to the topic, if the right approach is taken. Since it is an AA meeting, it's best to talk about the chemical dependency side of the equation first and the mental health side second. This simple change will make almost any discussion acceptable. Younger members of AA who have been through treatment are more accepting of these issues, and we fully expect that any resistance will fall away over time. After all, Step Two talks directly about AA members being "restored to sanity," so the issue of mental health isn't foreign.

It is our belief that the Steps hold promise for all of medicine, which will slowly unfold over the next few decades. Acute illnesses such as malaria are being conquered one by one. But chronic illnesses such as diabetes, heart disease, and addiction require changes in the lifestyle and habits of the patient. We think the practice of the Twelve Steps and the active participation in a recovery group are some of the surest methods available to make change happen and to safeguard progress made.

Families wrestling with co-occurring disorders need patience, courage, and tenacity. These mental and spiritual qualities provide the foundation for professional treatment and long-term recovery, for without them the treatment process may never begin, or it may bog down in the face of setbacks. It's often said in Twelve Step meetings: "Don't quit before the miracle happens." This can be difficult if we try to face both psychiatric and addiction issues by ourselves. Twelve Step meetings, both for patients and families, often provide the power to push on to higher ground. Never underestimate the importance of hope, faith, and teamwork in successfully treating co-occurring disorders.

Recommended Readings

Addis, Michael E., and Christopher R. Martell. *Overcoming Depression One Step at a Time: The New Behavioral Activation Approach to Getting Your Life Back*. Oakland, CA: New Harbinger Publications, 2004.

Alcoholics Anonymous. *Twelve Steps and Twelve Traditions*. New York: Alcoholics Anonymous World Services, 1981.

Amen, Daniel G. *Healing the Hardware of the Soul: How Making the Brain-Soul Connection Can Optimize Your Life, Love, and Spiritual Growth*. New York: Simon & Schuster, 2002.

Boriskin, Jerry A. *PTSD and Addiction: A Practical Guide for Clinicians and Counselors*. Center City, MN: Hazelden, 2004.

Bourne, Edmond J. *The Anxiety & Phobia Workbook*. 4th ed. Oakland, CA: New Harbinger Publications, 2005.

Castle, Lana R. *Bipolar Disorder Demystified: Mastering the Tightrope of Manic Depression*. New York: Marlowe & Company, 2003.

Duke, Patty, and Gloria Hochman. *A Brilliant Madness: Living with Manic Depressive Illness*. New York: Bantam, 1993.

Foundation Associates. *The Recovery Workbook Series*. Nashville, TN: Foundations Associates, 2004.

Greenberger, Dennis, and Christine A. Padesky. *Mind Over Mood: Change How You Feel by Changing the Way You Think*. New York: The Guildford Press, 1995.

Grinstead, Stephen F. *Freedom from Suffering: Seven Strategic*

Steps for Achieving Successful Pain Management. Unpublished manuscript.

Gronwell, Dorothy, Phillip Wrightston, and Peter Waddel. *Head Injury: The Facts*. New York: Oxford University Press, 1998.

Hallowell, Edward M., and John J. Ratey. *Delivered from Distraction: Getting the Most out of Life with Attention Deficit Disorder*. New York: Ballantine Books, 2006.

Jamison, Kay Redfield. *Touched with Fire: Manic-Depressive Illness and the Artistic Temperament*. New York: Free Press, 1996.

Jamison, Kay Redfield. *An Unquiet Mind: A Memoir of Moods and Madness*. New York: Vintage, 1997.

Jay, Debra. *No More Letting Go: The Spirituality of Taking Action Against Alcoholism and Drug Addiction*. New York: Bantam, 2006.

Jay, Jeff, and Debra Jay. *Love First: A New Approach to Intervention for Alcoholism and Drug Addiction*. Center City, MN: Hazelden, 2000.

Johnson, Sheri L., and Robert L. Leahy, eds. *Psychological Treatment of Bipolar Disorder*. New York: The Guilford Press, 2004.

Karp, David A. *Is It Me or My Meds?: Living with Antidepressants*. Cambridge, MA: Harvard University Press, 2006.

Larsen, Earnie. *Destination Joy: Moving Beyond Fear, Loss, and Trauma in Recovery*. Center City, MN: Hazelden, 2003.

Mark, Francis M. *Bipolar Disorder: A Guide for Patients and Families*. 2nd ed. Baltimore, MD: The Johns Hopkins University Press, 2006.

Marra, Thomas. *Depressed and Anxious: The Dialectical Behavior Therapy Workbook for Overcoming Depression and Anxiety*. Oakland, CA: New Harbinger Publications, 2004.

Marsh, Diane T., and Rex Dickens. *How to Cope with Mental Illness in Your Family: A Self-Caring Guide for Siblings, Offspring and Parents*. New York: Tarcher, 1996.

Meuser, Kim T., and Susan Gingerich. *The Complete Guide to*

Schizophrenia: Helping Your Loved One Get the Most Out of Life. New York: The Guildford Press, 2006.

Ortman, Dennis. *The Dual Diagnosis Recovery Sourcebook: A Physical, Mental and Spiritual Approach to Addiction with an Emotional Disorder.* Lincolnwood, IL: Lowell House, 2001.

Rome, Jeffrey. *Mayo Clinic on Chronic Pain: Practical Advice for Leading a More Active Life.* 2nd ed. New York: Kensington Publishing, 2002.

Solomon, Andrew. *The Noonday Demon: An Atlas of Depression.* New York: Scribner, 2001.

Szasz, Thomas S. *The Myth of Mental Illness: Foundations of a Theory of Personal Conduct.* Rev. ed. New York: Harper Paperbacks, 1984.

Torrey, E. Fuller. *Surviving Schizophrenia: A Manual for Families, Consumers, and Providers.* 4th ed. New York: HarperCollins Publishers, 2001.

Turk, Dennis C., and Frits Winter. *The Pain Survival Guide: How to Reclaim Your Life.* Washington DC: American Psychological Association, 2006.

Helpful Web Sites

hppdonline.com/index.php

HPPDonline provides informational resources as well as support for people with hallucinogen persisting perception disorder (HPPD).

ncadi.samhsa.gov/

This is the official Web site of the Substance Abuse and Mental Health Services Administration, a division of the U.S. Department of Health and Human Services. This site contains a wealth of information on prevention, publications, treatment facilities, providers, and statistics concerning addiction and mental health.

www.apahelpcenter.org/featuredtopics/feature.php?id=62&ch=5

The American Psychological Association (APA) has created this Web site to help people learn about mental health and how to find a psychologist.

naadac.org/documents/index.php?CategoryID=3

This Web site was created by the National Association of Alcohol and Drug Abuse Counselors (NAADAC) and provides information on the different levels of certified addiction professionals.

www.aapc.org/

The official Web site for the American Association of Pastoral Counselors (AAPC) can help you find a pastoral counselor near you as well as give you more information about the AAPC.

www.nmha.org/

The National Mental Health Association (NMHA) Web site provides a variety of information on mental health including help in finding a mental health professional, information on medications, and a screening tool for depression.

www.nida.nih.gov/

The National Institute on Drug Abuse (NIDA) Web site offers a variety of information about the different drugs of abuse, including alcohol and tobacco, and specific areas of information for students, young adults, and parents.

www.lovefirst.net/

This Web site, created by interventionists Jeff and Debra Jay, contains articles about performing interventions for people who have a problem with alcohol or other drugs, as well as resources and answers to questions about interventions.

www.arc-hope.com/index.php

The Web site for the Advance Recovery Center, which was co-founded by Jerry Boriskin.

www.alcoholics-anonymous.org/

The official Web site for Alcoholics Anonymous (AA).

www.na.org/

The official Web site for Narcotics Anonymous (NA).

www.bipolarhome.org/bipolar-websites.html
A list of Web sites about bipolar disorder.

www.marklundholm.com/
Mark Lundholm is a comedian who uses his experience of addiction and recovery in his performances.

www.emotionsanonymous.org/
The official Web site for Emotions Anonymous (EA). EA is a Twelve Step fellowship that helps people work toward recovery from emotional difficulties.

www.familiesanonymous.org/
The official Web site for Families Anonymous (FA). FA is a group designed to help people recover from the effects of a loved one's addiction.

www.al-anon.alateen.org/
This is the official Web site of Al-Anon and Alateen, which provide support for family members struggling with the consequences of addiction. The site can help you locate a meeting near you.

www.dbsalliance.org/
The mission of the Depression and Bipolar Support Alliance (DBSA) is to improve the lives of people living with mood disorders. This Web site contains information on mood disorders and how to find a support group.

www.moodswing.org/
Bipolar Focus provides information, education, and support for people with bipolar disorder.

www.draonline.org/

The official Web site for Dual Recovery Anonymous (DRA). DRA is a Twelve Step self-help program for men and women in recovery with a dual diagnosis.

www.codependents.org/

The mission of Co-Dependents Anonymous is to help people develop healthy relationships, particularly people who have a loved one with an addiction.

www.hazelden.org

Information about the Hazelden Foundation.

www.adaa.org/aboutadaa/Introduction.asp

The Anxiety Disorders Association of America Web site contains information and resources for people with anxiety disorders.

www.nami.org/

The National Alliance on Mental Illness Web site provides information, advocacy, and support for those living with serious mental illness and their families.

Index

anxiety disorders and, 48
depression and, 75
effect of, 31
relapse rate and, 31, 231
trauma disorders and, 156–57
itch idea, 174–75

J

Jamison, Kay Redfield, 85, 94
Jay, Debra, 27

K

kindling theory, 93
Klonopin, 56
Korsakoff's psychosis, 196

L

Lamictal, 95
Librium, 56
Lincoln, Abraham, 94
lithium, 89, 95–96, 97
Lithobid, 95
LSD, 114, 195
Lundholm, Mark, 169

M

madness without delusion, 131
malignant narcissism, 131
managed care, treatment and, 11
mania
    bipolar disorders and,
        100–101
        atypical bipolar, 91
        bipolar I, 86, 87, 88
        bipolar II, 88
        cyclothymia, 90–91
        mixed bipolar, 89–90
    manifestation of, 85
manipulation by addicts

of family members, 27–28, 30
of treatment, 22
MAO inhibitors, 56, 71
marijuana
    brain damage from, 196
    psychotic episodes and, 109
    schizophrenia and, 114
master's-level clinicians, 14
May, Rollo, 68
MDMA. *See* Ecstasy (MDMA)
medical doctors, 14–15
medications
    with abuse potential, 40,
        53–54, 56, 204, 205–6
    for anxiety disorders, 52, 54,
        55–57
    for attention deficit disorder,
        171, 176–77, 181–82
    for bipolar disorders
        setting off, 101
        treatment, 88–89, 92, 93,
            95–97
    for chronic pain, 203–11
    for depression, 66, 68, 71–72
    dosage, viii–ix, 38–39, 40
    early in recovery, 39
    misused, 18
    for psychotic disorders,
        117–18, 121
    for trauma disorders, 160–61
menopause, depression and, 70
menstruation, rapid cycling bi-
    polar disorder and, 90
methamphetamine, 77, 109, 115
mineral waters, 95
minimal brain dysfunction, 170
ministrokes, 190
mixed bipolar, 89–90
moderation management, 77–78

About the Authors

Jeff Jay is a professional interventionist, educator, and author. His work has appeared on CNN, NBC, and PBS, and in national newspapers and professional journals. He is a graduate of the University of Minnesota and a certified addiction professional. Mr. Jay is the coauthor of *Love First: A New Approach to Intervention for Alcoholism and Drug Addiction*, also published by Hazelden. His personal recovery dates from October 4, 1981.

Jerry A. Boriskin, Ph.D., C.A.S., has more than twenty-six years of experience as a licensed clinical psychologist, certified addiction specialist, consultant, national lecturer, and treatment program designer. He is the author of *PTSD and Addiction: A Practical Guide for Clinicians and Counselors*. A passionate advocate for integrated treatment, his vision anticipated the ongoing movement toward specialized and integrated treatment for co-occurring disorders, particularly those involving trauma. He has worked extensively with sexual abuse survivors and combat veterans. Dr. Boriskin is cofounder and clinical consultant for the Advanced Recovery Center in Delray Beach, Florida, a residential extended care facility for co-occurring psychological disorders and addiction.

For more information about co-occurring disorders, visit the authors' Web site at http://dualdiagnosis.info.

Other titles that may interest you:

The Dual Disorders Recovery Book
A Twelve Step Program for Those of Us with Addiction and an Emotional or Psychiatric Illness
Personal stories as well as expert advice offer experience, strength, and hope to people with an addiction and a psychiatric illness. Softcover, 254 pp.
Order No. 1500

Today I Will Do One Thing
Daily Readings for Awareness and Hope
This book of daily meditations is specifically designed to integrate recovery from addiction with the treatment of an emotional or psychiatric illness. Softcover, 416 pp.
Order No. 1400

Love First
A New Approach to Intervention for Alcoholism and Drug Addiction
Jeff Jay and Debra Jay
Intervention is the most effective technique that families can use to help a loved one suffering from chemical dependency. This book demonstrates how to perform a carefully planned intervention founded on love and honesty. Softcover, 288 pp.
Order No. 1203

Hazelden books are available at fine bookstores everywhere. To order directly from Hazelden, call 1-800-328-9000 or visit www.hazelden.org/bookstore.